Testimonials

"Vernon and Eli lay out in a logical order what is happening to our planet and how this impacts our health and well-being as humans. It is a must read for anyone looking to connect with Nature and make our lives better for future generations. We must take action now!"

Brook McDonald, President/CEO, The Conservation Foundation

"Being a Conservative most of my life and being an executive in a conservative, risk-averse industry, Vernon's and Eli's book gave me an opportunity to pause and to reflect on how the earth is being consumed at a faster pace than it can replenish itself. The book is a great tribute to Vernon's father and nature, and it will take all of us to help solve these issues. After reading the book, I went for a walk in a park to begin learning the language of nature."

Peter G. Bahner, Territorial Vice-President, Prudential

"Only by understanding and appreciating the natural world around us can we begin to make informed decisions about sustainable practices, policies, and lifestyles. Vernon's and Eli's book is a great introduction to some of the major things influencing the natural world all around us. He "connects the dots" and makes a convincing case for a much broader appreciation of, and connection to, nature in all its forms. As Vernon convincingly points out, embracing nature more in your everyday life can do great things for the planet as well as your personal well-being."

Jim Herkert, Executive Director - Illinois Audubon Society, Past Member - Illinois Endangered Species Protection Board

MAKE EARTH GREAT AGAIN

By Vernon LaVia and Eli Gonzalez

MAKE EARTH GREAT AGAIN

Vernon LaVia and Eli Gonzalez

Copyright 2019©

Publisher: The Ghost Publishing

Contact info: VernonLaVia@aol.com

ISBN: 978-1-7339405-1-1

Dedication

This book is dedicated to my father, John T. LaVia (1939-2000): English professor, world traveler, Shakespearean expert, visitor to every Major League Baseball stadium, and the smartest man I've ever known. He instilled in me a passion for discovery.

We were on Attu Island in Alaska when he died in my arms doing what he loved most, birding.

My mom, a retired elementary school teacher of thirty-four years, has this to say:

Johnny Tree

You were planted in the spring of two-thousand & four,

A small Blue Spruce tree, mere steps from my back door.

Your first visitors were Bluebirds ready to nest,

Soon, adorable Chickadees were the next guests.

A colorful symphony of birds perch in the summer.

Wintering Juncos love to gather in great numbers,

Connecting me with nature all through the year.

Your blue boughs and pine scent are so very dear.

Now my loving Johnny Tree is fifteen-feet tall,

And he stands strong season after season to welcome all.

In memory of my husband, Dr. John T. LaVia... truly a "man for all seasons."

Johanna A. LaVia, proud mother of the author

Table of Contents

Chapter 1
The Canaries Are Dying

"The forest and water problems are perhaps the most vital internal problems facing the United States."

Teddy Roosevelt, 1913 Autobiography

Your House is Burning

You may not know it, but your house is burning. All of your cherished possessions—your wedding photos, the pictures of your children, your own childhood albums, the photos of those loved, but deceased—will all burn up momentarily. Your favorite reading chair, your bedroom set, each of your flat screen televisions—including the big one—will melt and vanish minutes from now. Every physical item of value you possess will be destroyed.

The worst thing about this tragedy is that you won't have a place to call home for quite some time. You and your family will be forced to stay with relatives whose homes are ill-equipped to accommodate you. Or, you'll have to stay at a hotel or motel for a long period. Worse still, you might not have a place where you can stay at all, and a tent or homeless shelter will become your home.

While the insurance companies and the banks drag *their* feet and take a long time to help you get back on *your* feet, the outfit you were wearing when your house burned down will eventually wear out. Sooner rather than later, you'll be living in hand-me-down clothes from a thrift store or cast-offs from friends or family.

However, just when you thought it couldn't get any worse, something unfathomable happens. Your neighbor's house burns down, the big-box stores burn down, and your temporary dwelling also burns down. Before you know it, everything has burned down. There is no recourse or way to get you back on your feet because everyone is now homeless.

As you read this, you may feel a sense of relief because, hopefully, your real house is not burning. None of this actually applies to you. You and your family are safe in your home. The problem is that, one day, if things continue to go as they are, your house *will* burn—literally or metaphorically—as will every other house.

...if things continue to go as they are, your house will burn..

The Coal Miners and Canary Birds

Two hundred years ago, coal miners started to die from respiratory issues. The culprit, unknown for decades, was carbon monoxide (CO), an invisible killer that doesn't leave a trace. Coal mining was big business even back then, as just about everyone in cities depended on coal fuel. Arguably, the great economic nations of today were all founded on coal energy. If coal mining had stopped, there would've been catastrophic consequences for millions, and the advancement of industries and cities would have been curtailed. Luckily, someone figured out how to save people from dangerous CO levels. That knowledge saved many lives of coal miners and potentially many lives of people who were dependent on coal.

The solution was to encage canary birds and bring them down into the mines with the workers. When the smaller-lunged canaries died, the coal miners knew the invisible CO gas levels were becoming too high, and the miners fled from the caverns!

Birds, as it turns out, are the ultimate barometers or watchdogs, if you will, against invisible yet catastrophic natural occurrences that can wipe humans off the face of the earth. So, if you hear that birds have started to fall from the sky, dead, it's time to panic. Now, let me tell you this—thousands, if not hundreds of thousands, of birds have dropped dead from the sky. (AUSTRALIA: "Catastrophic: Thousands of Birds Fall from the Sky" https://www.wnd.com/2007/01/39632/).

...birds have started to fall from the sky, dead, it's time to panic.

- 5 billion Passenger Pigeons went extinct in a very short fifty-year period of time.
- 40 million Eskimo Curlews are now thought to be gone and extinct.
- 71 of the 113 species of birds in Hawaii have gone extinct! And 31 of the remaining 42 species are endangered or threatened.

The birds are dying.

It *is* time to panic. But ... from what caverns can we flee, and to where can we run?

Connecting the Dots ... AND... The Language of Nature

We, as a species, have lost our intimacy and passion for the earth that sustains us. After two-million years as Homo erectus and 200,000 years of living as more evolved, one with the earth—living on dirt floors, gathering/hunting our food, knowing how to gut a wild boar without its poisonous intestinal juices leaking onto the edible meat, plucking feathers from a bird or knowing when to harvest eggs from its nest, obtaining drinkable water, digging wells, and essentially understanding and speaking the *language* of Nature—it is easy to assume that over the last 200 years, as humanity has become "citified" (i.e. the result of mass migration of humans into urban areas), the language of Nature is becoming extinct for most people.

Many languages have gone extinct on the planet or have been lost to time. [See just one example here, with the story of the Native American Miami Tribe and their lost language, Myaamia:

https://www.smithsonianmag.com/smithsonian-institution/rediscovering-a-lost-native-american-language-4985160/]

But, if we continue to lose the language of nature ... because we think clean water comes from a metal thing called a *faucet,* or because we think energy magically comes out of something we call an *electrical outlet* in our home, or because we think a chicken never had to be plucked and is just something naturally wrapped in plastic on a Styrofoam tray ... we will soon risk extinction.

You may have heard a semblance of this argument before. Most people have. The problem is, many don't believe it. Some people conjure up images of tree-hugging hippies and dismiss the notion that the earth is being consumed at a faster pace than it can replenish itself. Some people think this message has a political agenda, so they choose to believe it or not, depending on which side of the political aisle they're on. However, those who don't believe it – purely for political gain – do nothing to help humanity, as they do nothing to change the way they live or help the earth.

In fact, in Richard Louv's book, *The Last Child in the Woods*, he cites a study that correlated how children influenced early on by nature became artists, and conversely, those who were not impacted by nature in their early formative years were likely to become business leaders and politicians. Thus, the very people who are in control of policy have the largest blind-spots when it comes to an inability to grasp the value of nature.

I'm a graduate of Duke University (cum laude '85: Economics), so, objectively, I'm a smart guy, right? Yet, I'm willing to declare that I am woefully ignorant about or have blind-spots concerning millions of things. I've tried my darndest to speak other languages or to grasp the theories of black holes in space, and yet, my brain simply seems incapable of *connecting the dots* for me to grasp those new concepts. But it's clear, I have a much better grasp on the language of Nature than the vast majority of my fellow *citified* friends.

In fact, I'm pretty sure Huckleberry Finn could connect more dots and read more signs in the natural world than a Harvard-educated lawyer/U.S. Senator today. And please understand, I say that with great empathy and zero finger-pointing. *Nobody can know what they don't know.* And most city folks who spend 90%-plus of their time indoors don't know nature.

> ...Huckleberry Finn could connect more dots and read more signs in the natural world than a Harvard-educated lawyer...

16

It's quite simple, really. Earth and its natural resources are the very foundation on which all of human successes, accomplishments, economies, and advancements have been built, and because most humans now live in cities, they simply have lost the ability to even recognize this cold, hard fact.

Thankfully, the voices of the few can still impact the many.

Heroes of the Past

We need more voices today, like those of John Muir and Teddy Roosevelt, who spoke out at the end of the nineteenth century.

Also known as "John of the Mountains" and "Father of the National Parks," John Muir lived from 1838 – 1914. As the son of a preacher and someone who saw God in even the smallest part of nature, he was an early advocate for the preservation of wilderness in the United States of America. We still feel and are blessed by the influence he had on policymakers of his day.

In 1903, Theodore Roosevelt wrote a personal letter to Muir to request that Muir guide him on a tour through Yosemite. Ranchers, land developers, and hunting/fishing camps and inns had, according to Muir's writings, destroyed vast wilderness areas for profit. According to Muir, they hadn't considered the long-term costs of the vanishing forests and polluted waters. The pristine glacial lakes of the Rocky Mountains provided great fishing for wealthy Easterners who could afford to vacation via locomotive engines, but their own feces and food waste were negatively affecting the very ponds in which they fished for meals!

Politicians of the time considered America's wilderness so abundant that it could never be depleted. Roosevelt wanted to see for himself, especially since he had witnessed the near-extinction of the Bison, the near-extinction of the Passenger Pigeon, the eradication of Elk and Bighorn Sheep from his personal favorite hunting spots, as well as the loss of 85% of all U.S. forests.

Muir loathed the idea of taking yet another government official on a camping trip, but Roosevelt had a reputation for being a rough-riding outdoorsman, so Muir hoped he could create an advocate in Roosevelt to preserve the wilderness. He re-arranged his schedule and wrote to Roosevelt, "I shall go with you gladly." And thank God he did, because the U.S.A. and even the world, which saw the wisdom of National Parks, has benefited greatly from that wilderness trek.

Roosevelt was true to his reputation. After the first night, he sent his men back to town, and, instead of sleeping on the forty, thick-woolen blankets they had brought for him, he spent the remainder of the trip sleeping on a bed of tree boughs like Muir. Rumor has it, he slept soundly.

Roosevelt loved Yosemite. Its horse trails, surrounded by thick ponderosa pine and giant sequoias, allowed the men to ride to Glacier Point. They were so high in elevation that the men awoke the next day covered in snow. Forest animals chattered along with John Muir, as he shared his knowledge about natural history and geology with Roosevelt. President Roosevelt finished the trip refreshed and enthused.

Upon returning to Washington, he used his State of the Union Address to actively encourage Congress to pass laws to protect Yosemite and other wild lands. He said they must be preserved because the great technologies and economies of the future could not take place without forests and water at the very foundation. He also created the U.S. Forest Service in 1905 to look after forest reserves. Roosevelt created parks and wildlife sanctuaries on 230 million acres of public land, set aside for the enjoyment and use of every American. During his presidency, he established 150 national forests, 51 federal bird reserves, 4 national game preserves, 5 national parks, and 18 national monuments! Muir's passion had planted seeds that took root to shape the American way of life, one that we still benefit from today.

By all accounts, John Muir and Teddy Roosevelt, together, had become earth's champions. Not only did they raise awareness of the importance of protecting the land, but then they personally set about to make a difference.

Heroes of the Future

My name is Vernon LaVia. I was six-years old when my ornithological fascination began, and it has continued for half a century. I've hiked and birded on six Continents, forty-nine countries and in all fifty states. I've even visited each Canadian province and I hope to get to my final continent, Australia, soon. I don't presume to be the next John Muir or Teddy Roosevelt. I certainly don't believe I'll become the President of the United States, though I was proud to call Barack Obama a personal acquaintance. He was someone who knew my children by their first names when he was in the Illinois legislature with my wife. But what I do know is that earth needs new champions: people who will defend and protect her.

...earth needs new champions...

We need courageous politicians from both sides of the aisle to come to earth's defense. We need businessmen and women to answer the call and bring awareness and charitable donations to help organizations who are capable of realizing that the house is burning all around us and know how to put out the fire. We need citizens of every country, of every race, who speak any language, to

20

collectively raise their voices and demand that those in authority do something to save our beautiful wildlife, birds, ecosystems, and ourselves.

If I have no one else, I'd love to start with you, dear and valued reader. Together, we can gather enough momentum that will shift the consciousness of enough people with the power to alter legislation and policy. Just as I am a smart person who admits to ignorance about millions of things, we need courageous leaders and stakeholders who are willing to say, "You are right, I don't speak the language of nature, nor do I understand how to read its signs. Please, show me the way!"

I'm not asking you to march, sign a petition, or video record a rant to post on your social media funnels. All I'm asking you to do is to finish reading this book. I promise, if you do, you will never think of birds the same way again, you'll never think of forests and wildlife the same way, and you'll never think of your role on this planet the same way.

Welcome to your wake-up call. The canaries are dying once again, but this time it's not deep in mines from an invisible CO gas, it's in ecosystems in just about every part of our natural world. And where can we run to now?

Please JOIN www.theMEGAmovement.org

Chapter 2
Loving Nature

"Man's heart away from nature becomes hard. [We Lakota] knew that lack of respect for growing, living things soon leads to lack of respect for humans, too."

Luther Standing Bear (1868-1939; Lakota Chief)

Powerful Binoculars

I was seven-years old, and it was 3 a.m. when my father came to wake me. He was startled to see me fully clothed and itching to go. He had been waking me up early for two years, ever since I was five and Jay, my older brother, was seven. We were explorers.

Well, not really explorers, we were bird watchers. Close enough. My father was fascinated with birds since around the time I was born. His father died during my first year of life, and a pair of binoculars was one of the items he'd left behind. While teaching English Literature at the University of Maryland and living in College Park, MD, he decided to pick up the binoculars and take a walk along the C&O Canal, perhaps to ponder his father's passing. As a group of four or five guys approached him, he did not know then the massive impact their chance meeting would have on his life, my life, and the lives of dozens of people I've introduced to bird watching. Those guys were members of the Washington D.C. Audubon club, and they soon pointed to a tree that contained three magnificently colored birds: Baltimore Oriole, Scarlet Tanager, and Blue Jay.

My dad was hooked! Those visual colors were better than anything his hero, Shakespeare, could describe in words. His life was never the same again.

My brother Jay and I never really had a choice in the matter. However, I would not have had it any other way. I loved nature and nature loved me. We were inseparable from the start. From a very young age, I immersed myself in nature ... literally. When I was six-years old, I buried myself in a pile of leaves in our backyard on Millbrook Drive in Willingboro, N.J. We lived along a creek with an eight-foot embankment sloping down to the water. I spent countless hours creating *natural aquariums*, using the stream bottom sediment to hand-dredge a small circular structure, maybe two-feet in diameter with six-inch walls that just barely broke the surface of the shallow creek. Picture a mini Roman Colosseum. And into to this animal pen, I would drop minnows, crayfish, frogs, and toads.

I'd scramble halfway up the embankment, through tortuous sticker-bushes, and bury myself under leaves as I learned to mimic birds at close range. And then it happened! The moment that hooked me on the natural world. A small brown bird, about four to five-inches long and weighing less than half an ounce, a male House Wren landed on the ground, five inches from my nose, and stared

> ...a male House Wren landed on the ground, five inches from my nose, and stared intensely into my eyes.

intensely into my eyes. He belted-out a song that shook its body from the end of his tail to the tip of his beak. He put 100% of his body and effort into a heroic display, as if to taunt me and dare me to try to take away his girlfriend (mate?). He shook and shuddered and danced like no other. It was practically alien. The song was a beautiful, trilling, energetic, flute-like melody, delivered in gurgling outbursts and repeated over and over and over. My imitation till this day pales in comparison to the real thing. Yet each time I hear the House Wren in the woods, I am drawn back in time to that exhilarating moment, buried in leaves ... at one with nature.

Exploring We Go!

When I turned eight, our family—my father, mother, sister, brother and I—boarded our VW van on the last day of school and headed out on our 2,000-plus mile trip to see as many species of birds as possible. Sadly, for my sister, she got carsick multiple times a day. So, before our first big adventure had barely begun, we had to drive back home. The following year, it was just my father, my brother and me. Mom stayed home with Wendy. We drove around the country for approximately fifty days. I found my place with nature. I appreciated her, I adored her, and I respected her. It was the best summer ever. I was learning the language of the earth.

During those early trips, my father taught me how to *get on a bird*—which is Bird Watcher jargon for spotting a bird—and then zeroing in on it. He taught me how to relax my eyes and focus on nothing and everything while looking for the slightest hint of what didn't belong. In other words, nature, its bushes, trees, and plants, have a natural way of appearing or flowing.

I became adept at using my peripheral vision and observing movements or shapes that didn't look like leaves, branches, foliage, or other signs of nature. I could pick up a twitch of a bird sooner than most. By the time I was twelve, I was getting on birds faster than people who had been bird watching for decades. In fact, I had graduated from a mere bird watcher to a birder. You see, bird watching implies a casual interest in observing birds around you, but to be a birder who avidly goes birding means a more intense experience to seek out birds.

Every day during the winter I daydreamed of the summer. We three explorers would talk about which National Parks we would visit and which species of birds we were expecting to see as we counted the days to the last day of school. As we grew older, Jay and I became members of the Delaware Valley Ornithological Club. *(It still exists today, and it's one of the oldest clubs in the nation, with its beginnings dating back to 1881.)* My brother and I were lovingly known to the older members as Rick & Rack. He was two years older than I, and we were inseparable. The more seasoned birders would send us everywhere like a pair of hunting dogs to flush out birds. No thickets or brambles were too dense for us to crawl under to get on a bird. It was exhilarating.

When summer vacation came to an end, my friends would return to school with stories of their one or two-week vacations at the beach or a lakeside cabin, or talking about the one day they went to an amusement park and rode a coaster. Then, I would wow them with my fifty-day excursion to all parts of the country.

One year, we'd leave New Jersey, drive south through the Carolinas, then cut west on our way through Texas and eventually to California, returning through Wyoming, Montana, the Dakotas, Illinois, Ohio, Pennsylvania and back to New Jersey. The next year, we'd do it in reverse. And the year after that, we'd go west through the center of the country and return east back through the center, but on a slightly different path. Oftentimes, we would enter Canada or Mexico. The journeys were magnificent.

Both of my parents were teachers, so I was a straight-A student. But to keep me focused on my studies, my dad would warn that if I didn't do well, I wouldn't get to go on the next epic trip. Even though I did great in school, nothing could beat being taught by Mother Nature herself. School and academia are linear and quite boring, with few moving parts. Conversely, there are thousands of random things, and life or death moments that occur in nature each and every day.

Even though I did great in school, nothing could beat being taught by Mother Nature herself.

Once, in a sixty-second span, I spotted a rabbit running at full speed, got-on five different species of birds, and watched an unidentifiable creature burrow into the earth to evade a snake. Talk about exhilarating! Another time, I witnessed an opossum give birth at the side of a trail. It's hard for city-folks to understand the level of excitement of seeing it in the wild versus on television. And, as the opossum was giving birth, I saw a fox race by thirty yards away and a baby toad crawling near the newly born opossums which, like all marsupials, had to make their way to their mother's pouch. Spring was in full swing, and I had a front row seat to its majestic performance.

After a few years of traveling all over the country during the summers, we settled into our roles. My father was the VW pilot and did all the mapping and planning. My brother did the trenching of the tent and clean-up after meals—a messy job, especially for someone who detested eggs as much as Jay. And I did the provisioning of supplies and cooking. We operated like a well-oiled machine as we zigged and zagged from Newfoundland, Canada to Key West, Florida. We meandered from the Atlantic Ocean to the Pacific Ocean and everywhere in between.

Teachers didn't make a lot of money back then, before the nationwide strikes of the 1980s, so we had to travel on a shoestring budget. We barely had the $6 to stay at a Motel 6. In fact, we would only stay there once a week to shower and wash our socks and underwear in the sink. Then we'd hit the open road again and camp at free rustic sites (i.e. "rustic" usually meant instead of a flush toilet, there was only a strange circular contraption sitting above a pit filled with very stinky human waste). If nature called in the middle of the night, I'd unzip the tent, then ever so slowly and quietly I would chalug* across the forest floor to the outhouse pit toilet ... for fear of waking my dad. At times, Jay and I would goof around as our father would converse with someone from a brightly lit, glass payphone booth, inquiring about where his paycheck had been sent. That telephone was often like an alien ship among otherwise pitch-black forests or campgrounds, and it created scary shadows and attracted thousands of insects that seemed to love my long, curly hair. I was too immature to realize it then, but now I can appreciate my father's tenacity to take his two young boys out into the wild every summer with less than $600 in his bank account

*Chalug: to walk carefully and as silently as possible over dry leaves, which had settled on top of a layer of wet leaves and dirt.

back home. My dad was a rare bird ... a brave risk taker ... a man for all seasons.

Our father took us out on these summer trips for twelve straight years. The smell of the outdoors, the food I cooked, and the myriad of mud odors while Jay trenched the tent were the best fragrances in the world. Ever since I can remember, I have found nature to be pure and welcoming. For the most part, the earth was my bed, the trees were my walls, and the stars were my ceiling. Life was great!

...the earth was my bed, the trees were my walls, and the stars were my ceiling.

But nothing beat getting-on the beautiful, graceful, yet fidgety birds. To see a certain species of bird for the first time was worth all the miles, all the desert-drive boredom, and all the muck and grime. It was worth the hours of trekking trails in silence, scanning the area with my peripheral vision, waiting to see a movement that danced to a different cadence of the wind.

Any birder worth his salt has a Life List, where you write down all the birds you've seen in your lifetime. Some people have 300, some have 2,000. I am up to about 3,600 species of birds, which includes about 800 in North America. One of my birding mentors from the DVOC, John Danzenbaker, died in 2008 with a Life List of 7,535. And during my travels, I bumped into Phoebe Snetsinger a few times, who was the first person ever to surpass 8,000 species. She died in 1999 with a total of 8,398 on her list (for a real treat, read her book, "Birding on Borrowed Time"). Now, with greater mobility and hand-held devices that can notify us of a rare bird sighting in real-time, there are eleven birders with lists over 9,000 species! (See the list of birders here:

https://en.wikipedia.org/wiki/List_of_birdwatchers)

One trick to seeing many birds is knowing how to call them in. The countless hours I spent outdoors allowed me to learn to mimic 300-plus species. Over the years, I got so adept with my impersonations—bird calls—I could go to a wooded area where there was no sign of any birds, and I could call in five or six different species, with a little patience. Many times, while on a walk, someone would say, "I'll buy you breakfast if you can find this bird for me." I was part human birddog and part bird-whisperer. Suffice it to say, I had many a free breakfast.

I became an International Bird Watcher. A gentleman by the name of Armas Hill founded a company called *Focus on Nature Tours*. I went on a few of his trips. Spotting a rare bird, deep in a jungle of Venezuela, gave me ten times the excitement any Jersey roller coaster ever could. When I was eighteen, I went on a trip to Kenya, Africa. Straddling the equator opens up one's mind in infinite directions.

Time to Grow Up

Unfortunately, life happened and I went to Duke University. Schooling and home visits replaced traveling the globe. After graduating with an economics degree, I got my first real job at Prudential Insurance. Citification started sucking me into the routine called *working for a living*. Instead of hiking for miles up mountains or down valleys, I was stationary, sitting at my desk for hours at a time. After the six-month training period ended and I became a sales rep, I was rarely in the office. I hated being indoors.

During my second year at Prudential, I became their top sales rep. When I was asked, "How did you do it?" I answered, "By being outside and not chained to a desk!" Birding inspired me and nature re-energized me. I kept a pair of binoculars and a bird guidebook under the seat of my car at all times, and in between appointments, I'd go birding wherever I could. I'd even bird along major highways, practically pulling my car into the woods to make sure I was safely out of harm's way, and then I'd just hike into the forest ... no trail necessary.

More than once I returned to the car to find a State Trooper waiting for me. They always looked bewildered when I emerged carrying a bird book and with binoculars over my dress shirt and tie, wearing big funny-looking boots that slid over my dress shoes. At times they didn't believe me, so I said they could open the bird book and quiz me. Some officers actually did. I'm sure my skill kept me from being locked-up at least two or three times, especially one time along the Mexican border.

I started to make enough money to pay an administrative assistant to handle paperwork that had to be done inside, at a desk. *Ugh.* Eventually, someone told my manager, and he called me into his office one day.

"Vernon, you can't pay Mary to do your paperwork," he said.

"Why not?" I asked.

"She has her own paperwork to do, and it's during work hours," he said.

"Actually, she does it after-hours or during the weekends."

"It's not fair to her... let her enjoy her weekends, " he said.

I responded, "She can stop any time she wants, she knows that. And my sales numbers are great, so what's the harm?"

He asked Mary if she wanted to stop, and she said it took only five to six hours per week to do my paperwork, and she really appreciated earning $20/hour to do it, which was twice the rate she was being paid by Prudential in the 1980s. She practically begged the manager not to stop our win-win-win arrangement. I won. She won. And Prudential won, because I could focus externally and sell more.

I worked there for a total of five years, with Mary doing my paperwork for the last four, before taking a pay raise and a managerial position at another Fortune 100 company, Lincoln National Insurance. I initially refused to take the job offer until they agreed to grant me four weeks of annual vacation.

After five years working there, I was offered a better and higher paying position at Aetna Insurance, another Fortune 100 Company. I held out for five weeks of vacation during that job negotiation. Only the CEO had more vacation time in the entire company! I was then earning well over six-figures a year, so I could afford to fly to more exotic places around the world. I then started to do many weekend trips by plane. I'd grown up traveling in a beat-up VW van, so I could easily drive my new car hundreds of miles with limited gas and bathroom stops to see a Life Bird.

In 1990, I met Linda. She was beautiful, and I made her laugh. I still love her laugh today! One problem: she wasn't a bird watcher. Something had to be done. I indoctrinated her before we got married. We camped on the black sand beaches of Hawaii, stayed in huts in Belize, coffee tree slopes in Costa Rica, and the Brazilian Rain Forest, to name a few. I had known she was "the one" from the night I met her, but when she bathed with me in a river where Piranha fish lived, I had no doubt! Our honeymoon in the Amazonian rain forest was bliss, even though we shared our hut with bats, tarantulas, and small frogs that would land on our faces in the middle of the night. Very creepy, but love was still in the air.

By age thirty-five, I had been to every state, including Alaska and Hawaii, and now I've been to forty-nine countries, and six continents. To date, I'm a serial entrepreneur, having opened nineteen companies, and I'm a serial bird watcher. I have found the balance between being in tune with nature and citification. [see the article in INC Magazine here: https://www.inc.com/magazine/20090101/passions-vernon-lavia-bird-watcher.html] Life surely has been grand, learning to speak the language of nature.

The more I travel and visit some of my favorite bird-watching sites, the more I hear of or see the decline of the space we once could roam. When I was a teenager traveling the country with my dad and brother, it seemed as if our boundaries were limitless. As I got older, I noticed more fences and man-made barriers.

I became more aware of the plight of many species of animals, namely birds, that have gone extinct. The more I learned, the more I spoke up, and the more I spoke up the more people started to pay attention. One day, I took a friend out to a little park. He was dumbfounded by my ability to get a hummingbird to come close to us, especially since that was his son's favorite bird.

"How did you do that?" he asked.

I said, "I mimicked the sound of a Screech Owl. The hummingbird came close to attack the owl because it feeds on small birds like him and its babies."

His name is Arthur Zards, the owner of TEDx in Naperville, Illinois. He said, "Vernon, would you be interested in doing a TEDx Talk?"

When I said *yes*, I had no idea how much my life was about to change, and that the MEGA Movement would be born.

Chapter 3
From a TEDx Stage to Writing a Book

"When we try to pick out anything by itself, we find it hitched to everything else in the universe."

John Muir, 1838-1914, naturalist, author, environmental philosopher, glaciologist, and early advocate for the preservation of wilderness in the United States. Also known as "Father of the National Parks."

If you're not familiar with TEDx talks, you should know that just about every person who wants to be viewed as a credible speaker covets the TEDx stage. In the words of the TEDx program, they conduct events organized by curious individuals who seek to discover ideas and spark conversations in their own community. Their mission is to spread ideas worth spreading to local communities around the globe. In other words, it's a pretty nifty thing to be asked to speak on a stage that many others are clamoring for. While I was certainly honored, I wasn't close to being ready.

Well, let me rephrase that ... in a sense, I was born ready... but I wasn't ready. Let me explain.

JTL Training

My father, John Thomas LaVia, was more than a globetrotting, nature-loving, bird watcher, and respected English professor. He had earned a Ph.D. in English Literature from Duke University as a young man and ended up teaching at Duke, Maryland University, and Rutgers, all very respected higher-learning institutions. However, as he became increasingly distraught with college kids who were, in his words, "unable to write a good sentence or paragraph," he stepped down from being a college professor and became a high school teacher. Even though some looked at it as if he'd gone backwards in his career, he just wanted to make a bigger difference in the lives of youth. He wanted to be able to reach kids at a younger age, before they solidified bad writing habits. *That* was my dad.

One thing he made sure to teach my brother, my sister, and me, was to enunciate properly. His pet peeve was when college students at highly-regarded schools would try to communicate a thought or idea, but they would stall and stammer and fill the void with *umms* or *uhs*. He wanted to ensure that none of John Thomas LaVia's kids were going to drive a teacher up the proverbial wall with such unfocused hyperbole.

So, periodically, he would sit us on a footrest, a padded round ottoman, and challenge us to speak on random topics for up to five minutes without ever stuttering or stammering or having more than a three-second pause. I'll never forget the time he gave me the topic of a *watermelon seed*, and how I reached the deepest levels of my brain to try to make sense without defaulting on any of the rules.

Perhaps I remember that particular topic more than any other because I was the big winner that evening. My prize—an extra slice of pizza. We didn't have a lot of money in those days, so to get an extra slice of pizza or to be given an ice cream sundae, when the other kids would get just a regular ice cream cone, was a big deal. Or, maybe I remember the watermelon seed because, not being the oldest, I was rarely the big winner. My brother was clearly the brightest among us, and my sister was certainly Dad's favorite. A win like the watermelon-seed win were few and far between for me ... but my tenacity never wavered.

So, in the sense that I can get up and talk intellectually about any given topic without flummoxing around, I was prepared for the TEDx stage. However, TEDx has their own ways of doing things, and it felt way out of my league.

I'm a member of the informal Interesting Fellows Club in Aurora, IL. We are a group of guys who enjoy a whiskey taster once per month, and we desire stimulating conversation that usually focuses on making a difference in our community. I met Arthur Zards at one of these monthly get-togethers. We had been sipping on a bit of whiskey and puffing on cigars when we came up with an idea.

Arthur thought it would be really cool if he could somehow film me and the surrounding woods to prove there were no birds present at that moment. Then, as I did my Screech Owl call, the camera would zoom in on the various species of birds that suddenly appeared and came very close to my mouth, from which came the sound of the owl. I have, in fact, had White-breasted Nuthatches get within six-inches of my head on many occasions. They can walk *down* a tree trunk headfirst, so I usually pressed myself up against a tree trunk to camouflage myself. And I've had Black-capped Chickadees actually land on me! And Ruby-throated Hummingbirds have hovered within inches of my face. The film would have been called, "The Bird Whisperer," and the plan was to show it in between actual speakers who appeared on stage.

However, not everyone thought it was a great idea. Allow me to draw the curtain and reveal to you some disparity among the bird watching community.

There are those in our community who believe bird calling is a controversial thing. The reasoning is that it may be bothering or confusing the birds and surrounding wildlife. By the way, I think there is merit to that way of thinking, which is why I don't abuse it. However, when people become extremists in any faction of society, their zeal and fervor actually can become a repellant to those who might otherwise want to join their group. In other words, we who love nature and strive to defend her can be the very ones who *turn off* the next generation from appreciating her.

In fact, author Richard Louv wrote a book, *Last Child in the Woods* in 2008 and coined the phrase, *Nature Deficit Disorder*. The book relates a story about a true account of an area where children were playing outdoors for hours, communing with nature, floating paper boats down streams, and catching frogs with their hands when "Private Bureaucracy" in the form of a Home Owner's Association created by-laws that, in effect, stopped the kids from going into the wooded areas. The children, accustomed to playing outdoors, erected bike ramps, put up basketball hoops, and did other things outdoors. Those activities were also eventually nixed by the Home Owners Association, for whatever reason. With the outdoors no longer a welcoming place to the kids and teenagers, they went inside and got fat!

It's taken me decades to perfect my bird calls, and when I'm leading a nature walk with Girl Scout or Boy Scout troops, or even adult groups, interacting with the birds is one way to show them the excitement of nature. It also demonstrates that we are not separate from nature

... but we humans are actually part of it! Nevertheless, for fear of backlash from many in the bird-watching community who would frown upon a video of me performing the song of a Screech Owl to call in birds to a very close range, we nixed that plan and had to go back to the old drawing board.

Arthur, the owner and founder of TEDx Naperville, wasn't worried. He knew I could enunciate well and get my point across. Apart from knowing me by spending time in our whiskey club, he had read the article about me in INC Magazine on how bird watching provided the balance that gave me the drive and desire to be entrepreneurial and open nineteen businesses, which provided the means to get out and into nature all over the world.

"At least when I get you on stage, I know you won't step on your tongue," he said.

However, for me, the pressure was on. Although I'm accustomed to speaking in board meetings, to groups, on stages, or as a guest on a television show, the TEDx format is unique. They give you a strict time limit of about fourteen minutes to speak. However, you are not allowed to draw any conclusions for the crowd. The success of the TEDx stages is that you—the audience—are presented with information and you draw your own conclusions. As an avid bird watcher and protector of nature, I felt that not stating a claim as a conclusion was going to be more difficult than doing an impromptu speech about a watermelon seed for five minutes without saying "umm."

TEDx Training

Luckily for me, Arthur and his team were fantastic coaches. Still, I found it challenging to come up with a topic that wasn't ultra-pro birds. Arthur and the women who worked for him and coached me, told me to try to find a different angle from which to present that would allow me to *put in a plug* for bird watching. One afternoon, having lunch with Arthur at Panera Bread, we were talking specifically about what to center my talk on when I noticed two people walking across the parking lot towards the Panera Bread. They were headed to a small patch of earth, about three-feet wide and twelve-feet long. It separated the parking lot from the sidewalk that led into the eatery. So then, the weirdest thing happened. Instead of walking across the small patch of grass, they went the long way around—to avoid it.

As our lunch continued, I saw a few more people do the same thing. "Do you see that?" I asked Arthur.

"See what?"

"Everyone walking in here from the parking lot is avoiding the earth. It's just like people who park their car in front of their house at the curb, and when they leave for work, they try to avoid walking on that strip of grass between the sidewalk and the curb."

"That's it!" he exclaimed, forcing me to look away from the earth-avoiders and at him. "You found a topic for your talk ... *Earth Avoidance!*"

We quickly cleared the table and went right to work. I started talking and Arthur jotted down notes as fast as he could. "Look at how we get out of bed in the morning. The first thing our feet touch is man-made carpet, which by the way, I don't think that new-carpet smell, regardless of how appealing it might be to some, can be good for our lungs..." Creativity and passion flowed at a rapid pace. I pontificated and Arthur scribed.

That afternoon, Arthur created a Flow Chart, took a picture of it, and sent it to me to fill in the blanks. Over the next two months—August and September 2018—I filled in the flow chart. From, *Earth Avoidance,* I got, *The Nature Gap,* and from there I got, *The Widening Human Nature Gap—a self-creating gap that has left us unable to speak the language of nature or interpret the signs of nature.* From there I got, *In Turn, That is Leading to Mass Extinction—the acceleration of problems caused by humans.* I finally concluded with: *AND ... All That Can Lead to our Own Extinction.*

As you now know, I was already an avid bird watcher and nature lover. But once I started to do some real research, not just for my own mental consumption, but to not make a fool out of myself in front of potentially thousands of people, my life's mission came into clear focus. I realized that humanity is on a fast-moving rollercoaster, but very few can see that some of the tracks haven't even been laid yet.

> ...humanity is on a fast-moving rollercoaster, but very few can see that the tracks haven't even been laid yet.

In a sense, I saw myself as a modern-day Saint Francis. He was the son of a wealthy merchant who had built a reputation of loving the most extravagant materials and of being an incorrigible playboy. One day, this young man who could probably have had the attentions of any woman in his city, suddenly gave it all up. The legend states that, at one of his father's big events, he took off all his fancy clothes and denounced his material possessions saying, "We don't need all of this. We see God in the bees, the birds, mosquitos ... everywhere in nature." From then on, he lived a life of servitude and in appreciation of nature.

Now, I'm a capitalist. I've owned many companies, and I am as much a man of business as I am a bird watcher. I'm not saying that I had an epiphany and was willing to give everything up to be one with nature. I liken myself to a Franciscan Catholic, and something had changed in me, and I was more ready than ever to be one of earth's champions.

The big TEDx day finally arrived. There were approximately a thousand people in attendance. Cameras were positioned in strategic areas where they would best capture the magic on stage to later publicize it over the Internet. In the last week, I had practiced the entire talk at least a dozen times in front of a mirror to make sure my gestures, facial expressions, and voice inflections were exactly how I had been coached. I was nervous but I was also ready.

When I got to the greenroom, I helped myself to the requisite muffin, cheese, and fruit display as other speakers walked in, some trembling with fear and others floating with confidence. The big mystery of the day was in which order we were going to go in. It was to be a game-time decision.

Like a whirlwind of simultaneous calm and activity, Arthur walked in and told me, "You're going second." He pointed across the table to a gentleman named Chris and told him, "You're going first."

Chris had prepared to give a speech on the tactics WWE wrestlers utilize to either incite the crowd or make them cheer. His talk centered on the power of

46

language—"I made you hate me today, but next week I'm going to make you love me."

When Arthur told Chris he was going first, he looked at me and quipped, "Don't worry Vernon, I'll probably do so poorly, you'll get a standing ovation just for walking on stage!"

"A standing ovation would be lovely," I joked.

A moment later, one of the women who'd coached us shouted, "By the way, instead of fifteen minutes, you only have fourteen!"

Whatever "cool" I had ... well, it dissipated at that precise moment. I had done two on-stage practices, the first was twenty-two minutes long, and my second was fifteen minutes. I had been in hairy situations before, having traveled most of the world and been out in nature as often as I have. I had even been bitten once by a **I had even been bitten once by a mosquito that gave me the West Nile Virus...** mosquito that gave me the West Nile Virus, which forced me to slip into a coma for nine days. I have had my share of nerve-wracking moments. But, as a semi-perfectionist, to hear that I had to cut off an entire minute from my well-rehearsed talk, just moments before going on the TEDx stage, filled me with a new level of anxiety.

I'm not one to focus on panic though, so I quickly thought of what stories or tidbits of information to eliminate. Before I knew it, I was being fitted with a lapel microphone as Chris was on stage giving his talk. I was suddenly walked backstage, shielded from the audience by long, heavy, black curtains as Chris spoke his last lines.

A moment later, he was done.

I walked out to the view of the audience and moderate applause. I had practiced my fist line over and over again, but for some unknown reason, in a split-second, I said something completely different. Dressed in a Joseph A. Banks shirt and a designer suit I'd bought from a thrift store, with a microphone clipped on, cameras pointed at me and dozens of blinding lights in my face, the juxtaposition of it all made me conjure up a thought, so I said:

"This is what a bird watcher looks like!"

It got a pretty good laugh. But, more importantly, it got an unexpected classic two-part whistle from a lady ...

the kind of wolf-whistle construction guys have been known to cast at attractive ladies as they walk by. And that whistle really made the audience laugh loudly. More importantly, that whistle calmed all my nerves instantly. So, the next line I said very calmly and coolly was,

"It wasn't the standing ovation that Chris promised, but I'll take it."

The audience rewarded me with another positive response, even though I just told them an inside joke, which by the way, I was coached never to do. But somehow, it worked. I waited for the audience to quiet down so I could get back on track with my actual talk.

That one statement about what a bird watcher looks like would go on to have a profound effect on me. But at the moment, I was centered on my talk. Then, I looked down in the front row and saw something for the first time that was not there during the practice dress rehearsals—a clock counting down the fourteen minutes! *Arghhhh!*

I proceeded to give my talk to the apparent delight and enthusiasm of the crowd. I ended my talk by sitting down and putting on an entirely different set of clothing over my business suit, kind of like Mr. Rogers putting on his sweater, and taking time to slowly do each button. I slipped rain pants on over my slacks, and then sixteen-inch high, waterproof NEO boots over my dress shoes. Then I put on my father's old birding coat, which is a color that blends into the woods nicely. And lastly, I put on a baseball cap with the word BIRDMAN on the front of it. I transformed right in front of their very eyes, and then prepared to walk off stage, as if to go birding.

Everything was running like clockwork, *no pun intended.* But when I looked down and realized I had two minutes left, I panicked a little and forgot to do the sound of the Horned Lark, a definite crowd pleaser. I forgot to mention that there are many "dots" to connect in nature to produce the "picture" that we humans may be consuming the earth at a faster rate than it can repair and replenish itself. I also forgot to tell the Canary in the Coal Mine story! Ever the order-follower, I finished at thirteen minutes and forty seconds to a rather loud ovation.

There was a designated area dubbed *the coffee salon,* where attendees could mingle with the speakers afterwards, and I was pleasantly surprised to see people line up to talk to me. Many were millennials, some who had never met or seen a bird watcher and others who didn't even know bird watching was a thing!

The wide-eyed reception I got furthered my desire to spread the message of Earth Avoidance and the Widening Human Nature Gap. By all accounts, for me, it was a successful night. When the video was released on YouTube and other online sites, and when many people who knew me saw it, I was bombarded with congratulations and questions or words of affirmation,

"When are you to speak again?"

"Everyone needs to hear this!"

"The human species is sleepwalking!"

"Your talk changed my life!"

"Bees are going extinct ... we'll go extinct, too. It's all about the bees!"

I Got a Guy

Many people, some who have known me for years and others who just knew me from that one talk, told me I needed to write a book. At first, I thought it was very nice of them to say that but then my mother joined the fray and it started to become more of a possibility.

"You're second kid is about to go to college. This has been a passion for you all your life, it's all you've been wanting to talk about lately, so now's the perfect time to write a book on it," my mother in Canton, CT said to me. She was a reading teacher for thirty-four years, so she knows a little something about books.

51

My nephew in Florida, Adem Aydoner, saw the video on YouTube and called to congratulate me. "Uncle Vernon, you should really write a book about this. Everyone needs to hear your message."

I thanked him and told him I was busy and, although I knew I had accumulated enough knowledge through my life's journey and studies to write a book, I wasn't sure how to go about writing one.

"Come to Florida," he said. "I got a guy."

I went to Clearwater, Florida and met, *the guy.* I was fascinated to learn his methodology and to know he had helped more than eighty people write their books. We spoke for three months, all the while I continued to get feedback on my talk and confirmation that I needed to write a book. After careful consideration and planning, I decided to get him to help me write a book. Eli Gonzalez is now my friend, and he has a new understanding of our human relationship with nature and the earth.

That's *how* this book you're holding came to be. Please, read on, I'm about to share with you the *why.* Go to www.theMEGAmovement.org to watch my TEDx Talk!

Chapter 4
Extinction is Forever

"Far less talked about but just as dangerous ... is the rapid decline of the natural world. The felling of forests, the over-exploitation of seas and soils, and the pollution of air and water are together driving the living world to the brink. Tens of thousands of species are at high risk of extinction, as countries are using Nature at a rate that far exceeds its ability to renew itself, and nature's ability to contribute food and fresh water to growing human populations is being compromised in every region on earth."

A summary of an 8,000-page, three-year report, spanning across fifty-plus countries and supported by the United Nations, it is expected to be released in May 2019.

The Passenger Pigeon

It was May 1850. Potawatomi Tribal Leader, Simon Pokagon was outdoors when he witnessed a remarkable natural phenomenon. *"It seemed as if an army of horses laden with sleigh bells was advancing through the deep forests towards me. As I listened more intently, I concluded that instead of the tramping of horses, it was distant thunder, and yet the morning was clear, calm, and beautiful."*

Eventually, the source of the oncoming noise that enveloped the great outdoors was revealed to him. *"While I gazed in wonder and astonishment, I beheld moving toward me, in an unbroken front, millions of pigeons, the first I had seen that season."*

What he saw was a flock of Passenger Pigeons, *Ectopistes migratorius,* which were, at that time, the most abundant bird in North America and possibly the world, with estimates as high as five billion birds.

Simon Pokagon was not the only one who immortalized the flights of the massive amounts of Passenger Pigeons. John James Audubon, whom the National Audubon Society is named after, also encountered an enormous flock of his own. He described it as thunder coming in the sky. In his now famous journals, he eloquently immortalized the passing of perhaps the largest flock of birds ever written about. The flock was so large it took a total of three days for them to all pass by.

At one point, a hawk attacked the flock, causing the flight pattern of the pigeons to change. Strangely enough, each of the birds that followed where the hawk had attacked, adapted the recently manifested elusive movements as if they were expecting the hawk to come back to the same spot.

John James Audubon estimated that he counted 1.2 billion birds in that flock. *(I'll let that sink in for just a second ... 1.2 billion birds.)*

You might think there's no way he could have counted up to 1.2 billion birds in a three-day span. You might be right. It seems far-fetched that any human, without the technology that was yet to be invented, could count so many birds in just one flock. But it might be important to note that Mr. Audubon had perfected the art of counting mass amounts of birds using only the human eye. It's a trick I learned when I was still a young bird watcher.

Basically, you quickly count up to twenty-five birds and mentally frame them in the sky. Then by visualizing the same size frame throughout the expanse of the sky covered by the birds, you can count much quicker by 25s—25, 50, 75, 100 all in three or four seconds! I used that same technique on many occasions, including once while counting over 15,000 Broad-winged Hawks in one day atop Hawk Mountain Sanctuary in Pennsylvania in the late 1970s

{http://www.hawkmountain.org/raptorpedia/record-highs-lows/page.aspx?id=349}, and during Hawk migration at Cape May, New Jersey in the 1970s, where they recently counted over 53,000 raptors!

[https://njaudubon.org/2018-cape-may-hawkwatch-53495-raptors-more/]

Mr. Audubon was not, however, famous for his method of counting birds. Actually, he was famous because of his bird paintings. And like many so-called pioneering geniuses, he really was just the right man, in the right place, at the right time.

Born the son of a wealthy French farm owner, he was snuck out of France with false papers—in modern times we would call it a fake I.D.—when Napoleon was unceremoniously *drafting* young men his age into the military to fight the British.

Legend has it that he got so sick on the ship to America that he nearly died. After being nursed back to health by two women in New York, he was able to connect with his father in the rolling hills of Pennsylvania. In 1803, he was a man searching for a way to make his fame and fortune. At that time, the wilderness of America was still mostly pristine and unspoiled. He noticed how certain birds seemed to return to the same spot on his father's farm each spring.

The concept of bird migration was still quite unknown, and

...the wilderness of America was still mostly pristine and unspoiled.

the 1700s had been dominated with theories that small birds either pseudo-hibernated underground to survive the brutal winter weather, or they hitched a ride hidden under the feathers of larger birds.

Audubon devised a plan one fall. He put a small piece of silver wire around the leg of an Eastern Phoebe (a species of flycatcher that nests in Pennsylvania), and the following spring the exact same bird returned to his father's farm. Unknowingly, Audubon had become the first "bird bander" in the world. So, with such a keen eye for his natural surroundings, he decided to travel throughout the great North American territory with the goal to paint every species of bird in the United States [see his 435 prints from 1827-1838 here: https://www.audubon.org/birds-of-america]

Folks were fascinated by the "great unknown" that existed west of Pennsylvania. And Audubon offered a tangible way to address their curiosity. He sold subscriptions to wealthy families on the East Coast and, with their financing, was able to travel more than most did at the time, sending about two paintings back each month to his loyal customers. He was ridiculed at first by bird scientists for attempting to paint live birds in their natural habitat.

The scientific way of the day was to paint dead birds, so as to have the time to paint every nuance and feather. However, Audubon figured it out and, not only was he the first to paint birds in their natural habitat ... using an intricate system of small wires to prop-up the dead birds in life-like positions ... but he also painted the plants they would eat, their nests, eggs, babies, and other details that his peers were not documenting.

While he and his paintings were famous at the time, in the burgeoning cities that supported him, it would be his writings about the birds that became more substantial in terms of his legacy. His journals documented a picture of America not yet seen by anyone, and his work would be cited by many over the next 200-plus years.

> ## John James Audubon moved freely around the country, never recording one moment of fear from Native Americans...

At a time when settlers' lives were in danger from Native Americans (Indians), John James Audubon moved freely around the country, never recording one moment of fear from Native Americans, even though he came across many tribes.

If someone were to have told Audubon that Passenger Pigeons, the ones he once counted more than a billion in a three-day span, were to go extinct in a hundred years, I doubt he would have believed you. But as the "White Man" progressed in technology and westward mobility, the billions of birds were cut to millions. The millions of birds were cut to hundreds of thousands. The hundreds of thousands were cut to hundreds. From the hundreds of birds, there remained only one Passenger Pigeon. Martha, the last Passenger Pigeon, died in captivity at a zoo September 1, 1914. Oh, how the mighty had fallen.

How could this happen?

The 1800s in North America was a time of bloodshed, expansion, war planning, inventions like the locomotive, and perhaps most impactful of all, city building (i.e. the citification of America).

Bloodshed

Once gold was discovered in the West, people who came to North America as immigrants, seeking a better way of life, migrated to the West in never-before seen numbers. The Native Americans, once welcoming to the newcomers, tried to stand their ground, as the White Man ruined their hunting grounds and became a threat. Blood and dirt paved the way to gold as many were killed and buried under the open skies of places that would later become the states of Montana and Wyoming.

Settlers systematically destroyed forests by building homes. The modern military destroyed more forests in building forts for protection. In addition to cutting down trees as construction material, miles of once-wooded areas were razed, simply so Native Americans couldn't hide in the nearby tree line and set ambushes. Capitalizing on their advantage by means of firepower—muskets, rifles, and canons—they deforested the nearby areas, forcing the Native Americans who wanted to attack to do so by having to first traverse a large, open field where there was plenty of space to pick them off using superior weaponry.

Expansion

After the Revolutionary War and at the end of the War of 1812, the terms of our treaties with Great Britain essentially allowed the U.S. government to defeat the Indians very quickly, without the English providing them with any food or weapons. The U.S. Congress took steps to promote westward expansion, and via the passage of several Land Acts from the 1790s - 1820, over 13.6 million acres of land was sold for about $28 Million dollars, providing much-needed money for the U.S. treasury.

[https://www.jstor.org/stable/25106763?seq=9#meta data info tab contents]

So, folks left the eastern cities by the hundreds of thousands in search of quieter pastures. Soon, homes began to line up, connecting cities up and down the East Coast, and eventually all the way west to California.

War-Planning

The American Revolutionary War, otherwise known as the American War of Independence, had ended in 1783. In order to win the war, the new America needed to stand up to the British in the open sea, something the mighty British Navy assumed could never happen. However, many miles of wooded acres were cut down in an effort by the United States to construct a superior Navy.

After the war, the American government vowed to control the seas with the mightiest fleet in the world. And when the War of 1812 started, the U.S. doubled-down and, made even more ships than they had during the Revolutionary war; ships, by the way, that were made of wood.

Inventions

Life-changing inventions were made, such as the locomotive. Before trains, settlers had to brave the terrain by horse and buggy, making trekking westward slow and difficult. However, once the tracks were laid and the locomotive connected the eastern cities to the western frontier, people started coming in droves ... literally by the millions. Historians and scientists may look back on this invention of "mass human mobility" as the moment in time when the earth could no longer replenish its natural resources at a rate that kept up with human consumption.

http://www.loc.gov/teachers/classroommaterials/presentationsandactivities/presentations/timeline/riseind/railroad/grants.html

Citification!

The first factory was built in 1790. By the mid-1800s, more factories were sprouting up and down the East Coast. The promise of steady work and steady wages was enough to lure hundreds of families to live near one another, and cities began to appear. Lumber of all types was needed as even more homes and hotels were erected. The furniture business, to build innovative items like portable chest of drawers, began to boom—which became another reason why forests were obliterated.

In the past 200 years, the U.S. population has gone from 6% to 81% living in urban or city areas. In other words, 81% of Americans now live on just 3% of the geographic land!

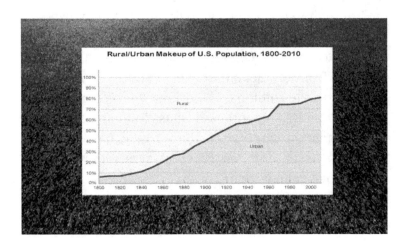

Bloodshed, Expansion, War Planning, Inventions, and Citification ... and pow! Just like that, the Passenger Pigeons were no more.

It is estimated that in 1840, as many as sixty million buffalo roamed the Great Plains, from Canada to North Texas, an area that covered more than a million-square miles. And during Teddy Roosevelt's life, he saw the mighty bison reduced to less than 1,000 in 1890. Going by some accounts, there were only 325 remaining by 1900.

...sixty million buffalo roamed the Great Plains...

(source: https://www.canyoncountryzephyr.com/oldzephyr/archives/buffalo.html)

In North America during the 1800s, times were changing too quickly in places that had never changed that rapidly before, giving the wildlife and vegetation no time or chance to adapt. Nature could no longer cure herself of the rapid spread of man. Natural wildlife paid the price for that incursion.

Chapter 5
The Language of Nature is Dying

"It is not the language of painters but the language of nature which one should listen to, the feeling for the things themselves, for reality is more important than the feeling for pictures."

Vincent Van Gogh (Artist, 1853-1890)

"Whether we and our politicians know it or not, Nature is party to all our deals and decisions, and she has more votes, a longer memory, and a sterner sense of justice than we do."

Wendell Berry (Novelist, Poet, Farmer)

Lost Languages

Language is at the very root of any culture or society. The way we communicate is extremely powerful, and it influences and reveals our values, attitudes, biases, and even our daily behaviors. We, as a species, have lost an untold number of languages. During the very brief history of the United States alone, we have lost many languages, including the many indigenous Native American tribes we had a hand in wiping out. As each mode of communication becomes extinct, so does the accumulation of wisdom that sustained them for perhaps thousands of years. Knowledge that cured

Vernon LaVia and Eli Gonzalez

illnesses, found water, and perhaps helped cope with pain through natural means, is now gone forever.

We all know of the majestic and durable pyramids that outlived their creators.

Knowledge that cured illnesses, found water, and perhaps helped cope with pain through natural means, is now gone forever.

Be they the ones built by the Teotihuacans in modern day Mexico (circa 350 BC - AD 450) or the Egyptians (circa 2,600 BC - 664 BC), those societies were vast and, I think any reasonable thinking person would declare, dominant. They built structures that could very well end up surviving the skyscrapers we build today. We are not certain about the methods or tools they used, but we can all reasonably agree they did not have the types of massive equipment we use now to construct such edifices. Although there are many theories on the demise of their societies, we have not found out exactly how they, the once mighty, came to utter ruin.

I bring up this point because the indigenous tribes of the Americas and the Egyptians most likely thought they would go on to live and rule forever. However, they, along with their knowledge and experiences, have become extinct. Their languages are no longer spoken into the wind.

66

There's another language, which I dare say is much more important, that's also starting to decline rapidly. And I don't mean Latin. It's the language of nature. As knowledge that once sustained entire races have become extinct, the language of life is also starting to disappear. We have lost the innate ability to understand this beautiful blue and green planet by its signs to find water, find shelter, find food, and find healing. Everything has become mechanized, robotized, and industrialized. In a mere three or four decades, our society has come to believe that pharmaceuticals, pacemakers and hand-held devices will sustain us, and magically the next great technology for our continued survival and dominance is just around the corner. We've been lulled into a false belief we can solve any problem with a handheld device or a corporate R&D budget.

Sadly, the Language of Consumerism is overpowering the Language of Nature. We are being stripped of the very thing that could be at the root of our successful survival as a species. (Chapter 8, "The God of Consumerism," will delve further into this distinction of language.)

We are being stripped of the very thing that could be at the root of our successful survival as a species.

In this book, we will attempt to connect the dots for you to paint the picture that we see. Do you remember getting those connect-the-dot coloring books? The easy ones were not as fun because you could tell the end-image without actually having to connect the dots with your crayon. We didn't get those. My parents got the difficult ones, so it would be a fun revelation, worthy of the time and attention to complete it. The picture we will paint for you, sadly, is not a fun or entertaining one. However, it is still worthy of your time and attention.

It's not an easy picture to comprehend, because you ... the reader... most likely are not fluent in the language of nature. So, the best way to see it is by connecting the many dots that make it come into view. We have to realize there is a myriad of variables to examine, to understand what many scholars, doctors, scientists, and ecologists, have been warning us about. The dots, in this picture-painting exercise, are irrefutable facts.

The Language of Nature does not lie. It is always truthful. It simply is. The distortion of truth comes when we attempt to overlay a consumeristic, ideological, or biased language on top of nature. For example, the language of nature would simply state: "Key pollinator species like bees,

The distortion of truth comes when we attempt to overlay a consumeristic, ideological, or biased language on top of nature.

bats, and butterflies are experiencing stark decreases in their numbers, with a generally agreed upon range of a 40% - 80% reduction." That statement contains no judgment. It points no fingers. If there are people who actually believe we don't need pollinator species to survive, then that is proof-positive we are losing the ability to speak the language of nature.

The data we present, taken out of context, won't enlighten you about where we will be heading if we don't take action. Also, if you only know a few of the facts (dots), it may not be enough for you to see what we see. However, once you see the many dots we present in the next chapter—the facts—and can, without prejudice or judgment, encapsulate all the information, I dare say you will see the hard truth that A) The Language of Nature is going extinct, and B) If we lose the Language of Nature, we, as a species, could be next to go extinct.

I'm not saying we will. I'm not crying, "The sky is falling!" So please do not apply your bias or interpretation that I am Henny Penny running amok in the barnyard. I'm just saying it's unlikely we will survive on this earth by not understanding its language. It's that simple.

Policymakers

The very people whose lives we depend on, or at the very least the quality of our lives is dependent upon, need to reassess their positions. They have had the luxury of listening to experts testifying in Congressional Committees on deforestation, over-fishing and over-hunting, the state of clean water in the world (with more than 3.5 million dirty-water deaths per year) and the billions of pounds of garbage dumped into our oceans. They have heard facts regarding the disappearance of salmon in Oregon and Washington, the plight of the Blue Crab in the Chesapeake Bay of Maryland, and the situation of sharks going extinct in the oceans for fin soup and false beliefs of their medicinal value! But, if they can't speak nature, it's as if they are hearing a Chinese person testify without the luxury of a translator speaking through a set of headphones.

If they can't speak the language of nature, they blank out. Additionally, because members of the U.S. House, for example, are elected for only two-year terms, as one Representative loses his or her seat to another, all those thousands of words heard in committee testimonies are lost, like one season of tree's leaves fall and yield to the next year's. And now the new, and often younger, Representative picks up the committee conversation midway—like walking into the middle of a conversation taking place in the kitchen at a dinner party. If you missed the first

And now the new, and often younger, Representative picks up the committee conversation midway...

half, you have no idea what the people are talking about!

It's just like that in Congress. But it's worse, because the younger folks are getting farther and farther away from nature. Their generation is spending more time indoors than their grandparents' generation. And it's next to impossible to learn the language of nature indoors. Finally, even if someone was raised on the land and should still be able to interpret the signs of nature, some leaders let their political affiliation trump even their basic need for survival as a human being.

We Need Teddy Roosevelt-Like Leadership Now

In contrast, Teddy Roosevelt, in his day, had fewer dots to connect. Forests were being decimated at an alarming rate, and people were getting sick from drinking water that was being polluted primarily by the locomotive industry, the textile industry, the farming industry (i.e. livestock waste), and by the amassing of people living on top of one another in cities. Today, our policymakers are challenged with thousands of unconnected dots, presented to them over a span of years. Then, as elections and retirements move people in and out of positions, many don't get to hear about all of the dots. Lamentably, this has resulted in the very policymakers, including past and present presidents, to talk unintelligently about the entire picture of nature.

I'm not finger-pointing or attempting to crucify any particular person or political party. I don't speak Chinese or many other languages, so I don't judge people for not knowing how to speak a particular language. I'm stating a fact—which is, while they have to vote and make decisions on so many things, it's impossible for them to interpret the language of nature like the experts who have devoted their lives to understanding the millions of moving parts of the earth.

Today, there are millions of corporations to police and govern, and each one is lobbying its local, state, and federal politicians to allow them to consume the earth *just-a-little-more*. It's virtually impossible for policymakers to connect the dots within their own political context, let alone within the broader context of the language of nature across all fifty states. Each request to cut a few acres of forest or to dump just a little bit more mercury into our waterways does not raise any red flags or sound any alarms for the leaders of today, who have spent their lives indoors and have become fluent in the language of consumerism.

So I get it. Even though they've heard the experts, what they've heard sounded foreign (i.e. crazy) to them, and it has spanned over the course of many years via thousands of pages of committee testimony, which would take a scholarly effort to synthesize into any kind of academic paper worthy of an "A" grade. Instead, they hear the much simpler, louder and clearer language of consumerism in the form of a corporation in their local political district, expressing the consumeristic need for jobs. In short, our policymakers have a fractured picture of it all and … well … it's just a mess.

I do not envy the role of a politician in our complex society where so many younger people have been raised completely separate from the earth and their natural surroundings. They have spent more than 95% of their lives indoors, and might define themselves by the dozens of high-end sneakers they own or the rack of 100-plus video-game discs they can pop in their console, (or the digital copies of games they download).

In one study, children aged ten to sixteen spent only 12.6 minutes a day on vigorous outdoor activity compared with 10.4 waking *hours* being relatively motionless.

[https://www.childinthecity.org/2018/01/15/children-spend-half-the-time-playing-outside-in-comparison-to-their-parents/?gdpr=accept] In another study, 62% spent less than thirty minutes per day outdoors (not counting commuting time). That's less time on average than an incarcerated criminal spends outside!

[https://www.hrreview.co.uk/hr-news/strategy-news/40-of-brits-spend-just-15-minutes-outdoors-each-day/111130]

The point is that future policymakers are not going to be any more fluent in the language of nature than our current policymakers, unless the demand to learn the language of nature becomes a top priority in the majority of households and educational systems in our country and the world.

We cannot allow their ignorance of the language of nature to determine the future of our children's children and the entire fate of life on this planet. The last great thing a president did for the environment was in 1970 when then-President Nixon signed the National Environmental Policy Act (NEPA) and, in that same year, he proposed the creation of the Environmental Protection Agency (EPA). You see, the book *Silent Spring* by Rachel Carson had been published in 1962, which alerted the public to the detrimental effects on the environment of the mostly unregulated use of pesticides. Congress spent the next few years reacting to the public outcry. Eventually, it was the U.S. House Committee on Science and Astronautics that discussed the need for a means of implementing a national environmental policy. In the U.S. Senate, it was the Committee on Interior and Insular Affairs that addressed similar issues.

We submit to you that the only reason there was such a swift and bipartisan response via the creation of the EPA is because Nixon's Congress was made up of members who were still much closer to the earth, having either been a farmer, a child of a farmer or a grandchild of a farmer. It marks the last time in our nation's history that a majority of Congress could claim to have spoken the language of nature with any fluency.

Not Optional

Saving nature is not an option. We should not be torn from any career gain, financial gain, or community gain at the cost of clean water or trees or breathable air. Teddy Roosevelt pointed out that we cannot have the next great technology without clean water and woods. President Richard Nixon was saying essentially the same thing. Roosevelt and Nixon were not against technology or the advancement of our economy. Instead, they saw that our society could not be great without the foundation of clean water, vibrant forests, and properly managed natural resources. We had just gone to the moon, so surely preserving the earth shouldn't be rocket science, pun intended.

Saving nature is not an option.

I'm certainly not a hippie, and I'm not touting any political party line. I've been a bird watcher for nearly five decades. I don't feel right if I don't get my dose of nature. There have been several times in my life when I was offered a mind-altering drug, and my response was almost always in the realm of, "No thanks ... I just need the drug of life from the great outdoors." When I spend time with nature, all is well with me. I'm more creative, more alive, more friendly, more appreciative of my life, the people in it, and what I've been able to accomplish. If I'm unable to get out into nature for a few weeks in a row, I get moody, tense, even angry ... and as a particular muscular, green giant would say, "You wouldn't like me when I'm angry."

After my TEDx talk, I met up with a Harvard University Physics teacher. She complimented me on the content, and then she said, "Your talk compelled me to seek out nature. I had no idea there were several national parks or recreation areas anywhere near Boston!" Can you see the irony in that? A physics teacher, particularly one who teaches at Harvard, should be an expert in educating others about our physical world. But nowhere in her schooling did she learn nor does she teach the basic language of nature. It is the very essence of physics! I believe that confirms my postulate that humans have simply lost the ability to connect the dots of our natural world ... even some brilliant ones.

In the next chapter, I'd like to play a game of Connect the Dots with you. It's not one of those easy Connect the Dot games; this is going to take some effort to ultimately visualize the big picture. But I promise you, it's worth your time and attention.

Go to www.theMEGAmovement.org to learn about Teddy Roosevelt, John Muir and more.

Chapter 6
Connect the Dots

"We are in a bottleneck of overpopulation and wasteful consumption that could push half of Earth's species to extinction in this century."

E. O. Wilson - Biologist, Naturalist, Author; often called "The father of biodiversity."

Like all modern day and past languages, the language of nature has evolved. It's had to, in order to survive. Words and concepts continue to be added and discovered, especially as new species are identified on the planet. But as there's been a dumbing-down of the English language here in the United States by the texting culture we have become, in a way, the language of nature has also been dumbed down, or simplified. It should now be easier than ever to speak it or decipher it. As our population has grown from 3.6 billion to 7.6 billion since 1969, the advance of technology and continued scientific study and irrefutable evidence has made the language of nature clearer to understand than ever before. Ironically, fewer people than ever before seem to comprehend it.

I will not boast about being fluent in the language of nature—very few alive are. I've spent at least 120 days per year out in nature for the past twenty-plus years of my life, but unlike the twenty-six-letter limitations of the English language, the language of nature seems, at times, to have an infinite number of letters. Even though it's gotten easier to understand, it's an incredibly complex language, one that has evolved over millions of years. But I do understand enough of it to know the message Mother Nature is shouting, which is, "I am hurting!" Much like you can understand when a pet is hurting.

Mother Nature is shouting...

You might wonder, *why does Vernon believe nature is telling him it is hurting?* Well, let's connect the dots and you tell me if there could possibly be anything else it's saying.

Like any language, the language of Nature has an alphabet system. As in English, Italian or Spanish, a letter by itself cannot paint a picture for you. You need to properly string letters together in order for them to produce words and then line up the correct words together to relay a thought or meaning. The language of nature is no different. If you examine any of these individual twenty-six dots—letters—by themselves, they won't tell you much. But when you put them all together, when you connect all the dots, you'll clearly understand the message nature is shouting out.

The 26

(These dots are not laid out in any particular order. They are numbered so that you can refer back to them and find the particular "dot" that may move or inspire you to look into it further.)

1. **Beavers:** (The second largest rodents in the world) The North American Beaver population was once estimated at more than sixty million. There are many reasons why it declined to just over three million in 1800; mainly humans: the White Man and Indian alike, hunted them to serve as hats or clothing. The beavers have seen a resurgence the last 200 years with estimations of a population of between six to ten million, proof the earth can be resilient if we humans get out of the way.

   Go to this link to learn more about how impactful they are to the earth's ecosystem: https://en.wikipedia.org/wiki/Beaver

2. **Bison:** Demand for the furs of these large animals skyrocketed after the decline of beavers. Once estimated at between fifty to sixty million in the year 1800, they nearly became extinct, reduced to as few as 400! There are many reasons why, including a drought on the Great Plains from 1845-1856. Normally, the herds would have been able to recover naturally from such a calamity. However, due to the

advancement of human mobility and hunting, the herds never had a chance to grow.

Couple that with the fact that the White Man left dead carcasses seemingly everywhere—as opposed to the Indians, who used 100% of the animal and then put their bones into pits to assure sanitation and a disease-free tribe—the carcasses became centralized locations for diseases, which killed more of them as well as other animals.

You can see a fifty-foot high pile of Bison skulls, as well as other great facts, at this website https://bit.ly/2v6QvF5

3. **Passenger Pigeons**: These birds were once considered the most populous birds in the world. The highest estimations were at five to six billion. They are now extinct, and most of their annihilation occurred in just twenty-five years, between 1875-1900.

4. **Rocky Mountain Grasshoppers:** Once estimated at twelve to thirteen trillion in the early 1870s, they were extinct by the 1890s. Scientists have concluded they had similar patterns to the Monarch Butterfly, in that they traveled hundreds of miles more than one time

in their lives. They would then retreat back to a central location, such as the Monarch Roost Trees in Mexico, to rejuvenate in semi-hibernation. (If humans were to cut down the trees in three or four locations in Mexico, the Monarch Butterflies may be next on the extinction list.)

5. **Eskimo Curlew**: This bird is now thought to be extinct, after estimates of having numbered forty million, and it was very closely tied to the Rocky Mountain Grasshopper, because, on its northern spring migration from Argentina to the tundra of Canada, it flew through the Great Plains of the U.S., and fattened up on the abundant grasshoppers.

Fun story. The bird's southerly 6,000-mile migration route took it from the East Coast of Canada, island-hopping across the Atlantic Ocean, down through the West Indies, down the coast of South America, and eventually to its southerly-most destination in Argentina.

On October 7, 1492, after being at sea for sixty-five days, and with his compass, for some strange reason, no longer pointing directly toward the North Star, Christopher Columbus was in jeopardy of a rebellion aboard his ship. His ship's journal recounts how a sailor suddenly sighted a never-ending flock of "shorebirds" (which we now know were almost certainly southerly-migrating Eskimo Curlews, mixed in with Golden Plovers), so Columbus made the decision to turn his ships to follow the flock! Five days later they *discovered* land! The so-called discoverer of America has birds to thank!

6. **Forests:** By the year 1900, 85% of forests had been cut down. 85% in approximately seventy-five years! Congress knew there was a problem, and, in 1876, the first forest management efforts began via the creation of the Office of Special Agent for Forests. The locomotive train and westward expansion, as discussed earlier in this book, made the problem worse. In 1891, the Forest Reserve Act was an attempt to withdraw some forest inventory from Public Domain. However, the problem got worse. So, in 1905, the management of forest transferred over to the Bureau of Forestry. It's crystal clear to me, hopefully to you, too, that if the ruling government of the time hadn't stepped in, the *Free Market* would probably have cut down just about ALL of the forests for things such as forts, ships, city houses, wagons, furniture, and firewood. Rain forests and northern boreal forests that ring the globe are under attack. Forests supply about 50% of human oxygen and absorb deadly CO_2.

This link will lead you to some great information on the state of the forests in the United States of America, including the estimate of only 7% of old-growth forest that remains here today: https://bit.ly/2XmNIUD

To find out the entire history of our forests, click here: https://bit.ly/2VRMmkq

Are you starting to see the picture these dots are painting? It's not that humans are bad, nor am I attacking the White Man, I'm simply pointing out the extinction events and near-extinction events that we have caused. Allow me to put on the guise of a translator for a moment. As any good translator does, I will try to just give you the facts. However, as most translators inevitably end up doing, I may add an opinion or two because, well, I'm an expressive and passionate individual and nature's cry is just so near and dear to my heart.

Let me continue to connect some more dots for you:

7. **Polar Bears:** In 2008, polar bears became the *first species* listed under the U.S. Endangered Species Act, due to climate change!

Click here to see why female polar bears in the Arctic are more frequently choosing to build their maternity dens on land, rather than sea ice because the land provides the stability and security that sea ice no longer can.

https://wwf.to/2tkRele

8. **Bats**: Some species have been cut by up to 92%! Go to this link to read how, as of 2012, white-nose syndrome is estimated to have caused at least 5.7 million to 6.7 million bat deaths in North America: https://bit.ly/2ZigZSc

9. **Birds:** The numbers of Bobwhite Quail have been cut down by 82%, and Evening Grosbeaks by 78%! In fact, in the past forty years, more than twenty different species of birds have been cut down by at least 50%.
http://www.birds.cornell.edu/AllAboutBirds/birdingnews/decline

71 of the 113 bird species in Hawaii have already gone extinct! 31 others are now threatened or endangered.
http://www.stateofthebirds.org/2009/habitats/hawaiian-birds

10. **Blue Crab** of Chesapeake Bay, MD: the population has dropped from about 950 million

to 350 million in recent times. Yet, as of this writing, the Maryland Department of Natural Resources is still allowing full-on fishing of the crabs.

In Louisiana, the policymakers have implemented a moratorium on fishing their crabs due to a decline in numbers. Click here to see how many local fishermen are crying foul for not being able to fish for them because it would limit their pay ... even though if they continue to fish for them, they'll go extinct!
https://bit.ly/2Go7rwl

11. **Ocean Garbage:** An estimation is that millions of animals die every year from plastic and garbage created by humans; birds, mammals, fish, coral, and probably the extinction of animals yet to be identified.

We are not halfway through connecting the dots or learning Nature's *alphabet* system. Still, let me ask you, is the picture becoming clearer? Are you understanding what Nature is screaming to us? Let's continue on, it gets better ... I mean, worse.

12. **Clean Water Issues**: the next chapter will cover the Greatness of Water. Suffice it to say that we are taking in drinkable water, mixing in heavy

metals and chemicals that are not being taken back out by our municipal water reclamation districts, so we are not returning as much drinkable water to the earth as we are using.

13. **Ozone Hole over Argentina / Antarctica**: There is a lot of mis-information about this topic. What most experts agree on is that it's been a natural occurrence for an estimated 500 years, re-appearing each year for a period of time. However, the issue is the *thinning* of the ozone or the larger size of the hole when it does appear. It is believed by many experts that the man-made chemicals and pollutants are what is causing the thinning ozone.

Go to this link to see how the Ozone has expanded to be four times the size of Australia: https://ab.co/2VSQ11d

14. **Bramble Cay Melomys** (Australian Rodent): In February 2019, it became the first mammal declared extinct due to climate change!

(I purposefully wrote this dot to be short because it's so powerful, please, read it again.)

15. **Mammals of Great Britain**: An estimated one in five will be extinct within ten years!

    Go to this link for more details:
    https://bit.ly/2GsSCts

16. **Bees!** What if I told you that the number of Honey Bee colonies shrank by 59% from 1945 - 2005? Or that they shrank by 42%, from 4.1 million to 2.4 million from 1978 - 2006? And what if I were to tell you that population of bees had further decreased by another 40% since 2006? Would it worry you? Would you even *bee-lieve* it?

    [http://sos-bees.org/situation/]

    It is commonly believed that if the bees go extinct, human population would diminish greatly via massive famines and wars over food supply, because about 40% of all human food is pollinated by bees, bats, birds, and butterflies ... but mostly bees. And those foods contain flavonoids and minerals that humans must have, and those elements are not contained in the wind-pollinated food sources like grains and grasses.

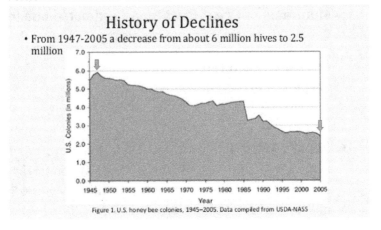

Figure 1. U.S. honey bee colonies, 1945–2005. Data compiled from USDA-NASS

To copy the line from the popular Verizon television commercials, "Can you hear me now?" There are no reasonable ways to argue against facts. The world's top experts, people who have dedicated their lives to understanding our planet, have largely come together to help us connect earth's language dots in order to understand her message. But wait, she's not done talking to us.

17. **Salmon:** (I'm using salmon as a representative of the many fish that are threatened.) Two species of Chinook Salmon are listed as endangered under the Endangered Species Act (ESA). Another seven species are listed as threatened and one is a candidate for listing. If these fish, which are instrumental to our ecosystem, are killed off, everything will change.

Go to this link for more details:
https://bit.ly/2vgNkL5

18. **All Mammals Larger than Cows**: A study, led by University of Mexico biologist, Felisa Smith, states the probability that all mammals larger than cows could go extinct between 2030–2050, including the largest mammal, the elephant.

Go to this link for more details:
https://bit.ly/2KX6gcE

19. **Shark Extinction**: Seventeen of thirty-nine species of sharks are on the brink of extinction! They are one of the oldest species on the planet, with fossil records of 400 million years. They have outlived dinosaurs and probably hundreds of *mass extinction* events, but just about all evidence points to them not surviving the *human hunter & nature destroyer.*

The sad part about over-hunting sharks is most of it is done with the false belief that the fins provide nutritional health value to humans. They don't.

Click here to find out more about the shark species: https://wwf.to/2E2JyHr

20. **Rain Forests**—the "Lungs of the Planet." It is estimated that 150 acres of forests are cut down every minute. That's 78-million acres that are cut down per year!

20% of the Amazon Rain Forest has disappeared in the past 50–75 years. As if that's not troubling enough, the rate of its disappearance has increased! As an aside, but certainly a part of this topic, the human population has doubled in that period of time.

Click here to find out how important the rain forest is, just for medicinal purposes: www.rain-tree.com

21. **Species Extinction**: is up 1,000 times, due to humans, as written in the May 29, 2014 issue of the Journal of Science.

As many as 1.9 million species are threatened. Allow that massive number to permeate your consciousness—1.9 million—threatened to become extinct.

Click here to find out more on how species extinction is happening a thousand times faster because of humans: https://bit.ly/2yR9FhR

If that isn't bad enough, click here to read how up to 50% of all species could go extinct by the year 2050, unless humanity addresses man-made climate change, according to biologists: https://bit.ly/2DFcd7R

22. Sea Levels are Rising and Heating-Up:

https://www.wunderground.com/cat6/Highest-Sea-Level-Rises-US-are-Texas-and-Louisiana-Annual-Report-Finds

This is a confusing topic for most folks. I get it. In some places, levels are not rising and in others they are. Some reports talk of such miniscule increases in sea levels each year that most of us can't fathom how a mere half-inch over the next few decades could amount to a problem. It's incredibly complex. So, let's look at just two "real" things going on in the world: Palau and submarines.

My good friend, Rudy Rodriguez, was on Necker Island with billionaire Richard Branson when his non-profit organization, "Ocean United," kicked off their 30X30 campaign to preserve and restore 30% of the ocean by the year 2030. And one day Rudy had a meal with the President of Palau, a nation in the western Pacific Ocean, made up of about 340 islands. The president told him that he has lost 30%-40% of his nation due to rising oceans! Can you imagine ... you get elected as president of a nation in the year 2000, and then you find out you have less than two-thirds of the land left on which to serve as its leader? In an article (see link below), Palau's president recounts how he had to adapt to the rising seas that caused tidal salt water to wipe out his wife's flower gardens. Now they must put their flowers in pots, which are raised above the new, higher sea level.

https://www.independent.co.uk/news/world/australasia/climate-change-south-pacific-global-warming-sea-levels-a7829786.html

Okay ... so a minor adaptation like spending money on raised flower pots may not seem important (of course those flowers help keep our food-pollinators alive), but what if an adaptation cost $32 billion ... would that get your attention? Well, ice melting and sea levels rising is, indeed, related to submarines. Yes ... I said *submarines*.

You may think this is a strange "dot" to connect to the rest. But our military leaders told Congress they needed ten more submarines to patrol the newly de-iced ocean expanses of the world in the Arctic. At a cost of $32 billion dollars, the impact of climate change is expensive. In fact, it was my very own Navy

League Club of Aurora, IL, that petitioned the President of the United States to name one of the Virginia Class nuclear subs the "USS Illinois." It was the first Navy fleet vessel to be named after my state, Illinois, in over 100 years. Then in October 2015, I had a front-row seat at the Naval Submarine Base, New London, Connecticut when the First Lady of the United States christened it and broke the Champagne bottle on its bow.

https://en.m.wikipedia.org/wiki/USS_Illinois_(SSN-786)

23. **Ice Age:** Wow ... when was the last time you were at a friend's house for a BBQ or at a restaurant with friends, and someone said, "Boy ... how about that ice age that's coming?" May sound silly, but believe it or not, science has been predicting the next ice age since the late 1800s and, by most predictions, it will happen at some point in the next 1,500-50,000 years.

In a published article (see link below) a former NASA scientist has said the next ice age is predicted to begin anytime from 40 years to 60,000 years! Okay ... that may seem like a crazy large time span. However, for many years, most of science has agreed with the prediction that the next ice age is likely to start anytime from the next 1,500 years–50,000 years. So ... it's possible, that the massive effects on the earth over the past fifty years that our book highlights "could" be the thing that accelerates the coming of the next ice age.

That's why I believe Geothermal and Hydrogen Energy needs to be the big investment. The earth's core temperature will not change. But, wind, solar, hydro, oil, and even natural gas could either run out, or become too difficult or random to harness during an ice age to help human survival.

https://www.express.co.uk/news/science/1121 903/nasa-news-scientist-ice-age-antarctica-find-this-date-spt

24. **Krill:** The trillions of krill that inhabit the southern oceans are down by 40% - 80% since the 1970s. In many ways, all life on the planet is dependent on these little guys, since millions of fish eat them, including the largest, who eat them by the thousands each day.

https://www.theguardian.com/environment/20 18/feb/14/decline-in-krill-threatens-antarctic-wildlife-from-whales-to-penguins

25. **Anchovy:** Similar to the declines in Krill, these fish are vital as a food source for so many larger animals. Their numbers are also down between 40%-80% since the 1970s.

https://environment-review.yale.edu/mortality-and-starvation-wildlife-could-anchovies-be-cause-0

26. **Phytoplankton:** 50% of our oxygen comes from these, mostly, single-celled plants that reside in the vast oceans. All life depends on phytoplankton. Sadly, estimates put their decline at 20% - 40% due to hotter waters, less iron-rich poop from fish and whales, and our discarded garbage.

https://www.newscientist.com/article/dn18807-whale-poop-is-vital-to-oceans-carbon-cycle/

All life depends on phytoplankton ... even HUMAN life.

https://www.scientificamerican.com/article/phytoplankton-population/

http://blueplanetsociety.org/2016/02/whats-happening-to-oceans-phytoplankton/

I will stop here, at 26 dots, to emphasize that the English language has only 26 letters in its alphabet. But the language of Nature has an enormous amount of letters, perhaps an infinite amount, in its alphabet.

I implore you to allow yourself to take in this information without bias or prejudice. I'm talking about nothing less than massive, worldwide, biblical-proportion-type species going extinct!!! I apologize for my usage of exclamation points. As most people know, in the texting culture, the usage of an exclamation point is symbolic of someone yelling. I'm not yelling. I'm simply translating the message. It's the sound of all the threatened species that are yelling.

Allow me to recap these 26 dots:

1. Beavers

2. Bison

3. Passenger Pigeons

4. Rocky Mountain Grasshoppers

5. Eskimo Curlew

6. Forests

7. Polar Bears

8. Bats

9. Birds

10. Blue Crab

11. Ocean Garbage

12. Clean Water

13. Ozone Hole

14. Bramble Cay Melomys

15. Mammals of Great Britain

16.   Bees

17.   Salmon

18.   All mammals larger than cows

19.   Shark extinction

20.   Rain Forests

21.   Extinction of thousands of species projected!

22.   Sea levels rising

23.   Ice Age

24.   Krill

25.   Anchovy

26.   Phytoplankton

These 26, in my opinion, should make any reasonable-thinking person evaluate his or her role as stewards to this beautiful green and blue planet we live on. Earth Avoidance and Citification are huge players in this macabre game of life and death.

I don't care what side of the political aisle you're on, we all need to come together to create a massive paradigm shift. I, Vernon LaVia, and my co-author, Eli Gonzalez, sit on opposite sides of the political spectrum. However, we have come together, leaving political rhetoric aside, to bring you this somber news: our earth is dying, as are her inhabitants.

It's time for action. In the last chapter of this book, we're going to show you how you—dear and valued reader—not your neighbor, not your church, not your rotary club, and not your political party—how YOU can help us join a grass roots movement that will change the trajectory of our existence on this planet. If many experts' predictions are correct, we have precious little time left on this earth before we, too, join the extinction list.

Learn more about the 26 at
www.theMEGAmovement.org.

Chapter 7
Water Made America Great

"Water is life's matter and matrix, mother and medium. There is no life without water."

Albert Szent-Gyorgyi, Hungarian biochemist and Nobel Prize Winner for Medicine.

"The wars of the twenty-first century will be fought over water."

Ismail Serageldin, World Bank Vice President for Environmental Affairs

The earth might seem like it has abundant water but, in fact, less than 1% is available for human use. The rest is either salt water found in oceans, fresh water frozen in the polar ice caps, or too inaccessible for practical usage. While population and demand on freshwater

...less than 1% is available for human use.

resources are increasing, supply on planet earth will always remain constant. And although it's true that the water cycle continuously returns water to earth, it is not always returned to the same place, or in the same quantity and quality. We take water from earth's fresh sources, but after it goes down our sinks, toilets, and factory drains, it ends up at municipal water reclamation facilities, which do their best to process and clean it before returning it to rivers, lakes, and reservoirs. The problem is that we are adding heavy metals, pesticides, and estrogen ... among other things ... that are NOT being taken out of the water because it would cost billions, if not trillions of dollars to do so. Here's a list of some items that have been found in the drinking water in cities:

DEET	Acesulfame-K	BPA
Atrazine	Cyanazine	Diltiazem
Nicotine	Atenolol	Sulfadiazine
DEA	Furosemide	Theobromine
Sulfamethoxazole	Caffeine	Ibuprofen
DACT	Gemfibrozil	Iopromide
DIA	Cis-Testosterone	Ketoprofen
Cotinine	TBEP	Trans-
Testosterone	Progesterone	Simazine
PFOS	2,4-D	TCEP
Meprobamate	Phenytoin	
Acetaminophen	Dehydronifedipine	
Methadone		

Water, when it flows, is alive. The water, itself, is a miraculous concoction of hydrogen and oxygen balanced perfectly to create the fluid solution that gives and sustains life. In addition to those molecules, however, are minute organisms, minerals, and inert properties that make up the water we find on our earth. The proportion and

Water, when it flows, is alive.

kinds of organisms, minerals, etc., depends on where the water is found.

Wherever water is, life will converge—teeming around it. Well, let's be clear: wherever clean water is found, life is found. Unclean water can be deadly. In fact, about four-million people per year are still dying on this planet from unsafe drinking water.

Henny Penny Time

Imagine, for just a moment, what would happen if earth's drinkable water supply shrank by 60%? Let's suppose all drinkable water in Illinois was gone. Do you believe the people from my great state would just slip quietly into the night without a fight? Would you think it reasonable or plausible that the law-abiding citizens of the state of Pennsylvania would complacently watch their children die from dehydration, knowing there's drinkable water available in New Jersey? Do you believe the law-abiding citizens of New Jersey would openly welcome the millions of Philadelphians into their territory to drink the only water they and their families have, when their survival depends on it?

The way I envision it is terrifying.

I see blood on the streets of every country. I see riots, murders, anarchy, and massive upheavals of political power. I see power failure, the strong taking from the weak, extortion, Marshall Law, massive invasions of millions of people into countries where clean water exists. To a great extent, it would be the end of civility.

Basically, I see an overall collapse of society as we know it. What do you see?

In the previous chapter you read on how forests have been decimated, many species have decreased by more than 50%, many other species have become extinct. Climate change is a fact. It is not inconceivable to think of a near future – 20 to 40 years – where our water supply has diminished by a large percentage. What then? What type of future would your children have?

Join the MEGA Movement,
www.theMEGAmovement.org.

Chapter 8
The New God

Fifty years ago we finally ventured to the moon. For the very first time we looked back and saw our blue planet. Since then, our population has more than doubled...[and]now, in the space of just one human lifetime ... wildlife populations have, on average, declined by 60%. For the first time in human history, the stability of nature can no longer be taken for granted.

David Attenborough (2019, "Our Planet")

"Consumerism is a great disease today. I am not saying that we all do this, no. But consumerism, spending more than we need, is a lack of austerity in life; this is an enemy of generosity."

Pope Francis (Nov. 26, 2018, during Mass at Domus Sanctae Marthae, Rome)

Throughout the history of humanity, we, as a species, have mostly believed in a higher power. Since men learned to paint a picture in caves, images of beings greater than ourselves were drawn. Many great wars were fought, and an untold number of people died in the name of God or religion. Also, many great, selfless, and historic deeds were done to "love-thy-neighbor" in the name of God or religion. Religion is so embedded in our society, when an atheist is about to crash or hears some unexpected news, he or she says, "Oh, my God!"

This country, in particular, the United States of America, was founded upon Christian biblical principles. There are millions of people who still believe in those foundational *truths,* and many more believe in another *truth (i.e. various religions)*, while the afore-mentioned atheists profess to believe in nothing at all. And before Europeans arrived, the indigenous people worshipped a Great Spirit ... one could say it was Mother Nature herself.

However, all of us are now bowing down to a new deity. You won't find *spirit-filled* texts written about him. You won't find a congregation to sit down and worship him. You won't go through any ritual rites of passages because of him, either. In fact, although we all seek him, we don't adore him or call him by name, because his most significant achievement is remaining invisible. He is the *god of consumerism.*

The God of Consumerism

Consumerism: the protection of the rights and interests of the general pool of buyers, or an obsession with buying material goods or items.

The things we purchase have become the main focus of many people's lives. We no longer try to *keep up with the Joneses*; we all want to be better than the Joneses.

Our need for better is an addiction; a better watch, a better car, a better lamp, a better wardrobe, a better this and a better that, has given consumerism a following so blind and loyal, all of the other gods must be jealous. This apparent need for always wanting the newest and the best has driven technology to the point where we stop asking if we should even continue doing something. Instead, we just want to know if people will buy it.

...we all want to be better than the Joneses...

The ingenuity of man continues to grow and amaze the masses of people with money, debit cards, credit cards, cryptocurrency like Bitcoin, and even those who wish to barter. We now put more faith in capitalism and consumerism than church itself, and it trumps our faith in who we profess to believe in. For example, we blindly believe medical technology and medicine will find the next great cure ... just around the corner. Sure, we'll still pray for your sick son, but first give him $millions of dollars$ of medical care. You know ... just in case God needs help, *wink, wink.* And it's clear to me that more people go shopping on the holy days than those who go to church, temple, mosque or another place of worship.

My dear friend Mavis Bates, a college teacher of Sustainability, and an owner of a business for fifteen-plus years suggested: "In order to have sustainable businesses we must have a sustainable environment. In other words, right now we are consuming the earth's natural resources ... including trees, water, and oxygen ... at a pace that is faster than nature can replenish itself." I've opened over a dozen businesses. She and I are NOT anti-business or against capitalism. On the contrary, we simply see the inherent flaws and inefficiencies with today's corporate structure, where

> **...we are consuming the earth's natural resources ... including trees, water, and oxygen ... at a pace that is faster than nature can replenish itself.**

the "FREE" stuff they get from nature is simply not valued, and therefore it is being squandered and turned into garbage ... no "fault" of anyone, really. It's just the process we've come to believe is the most economical way to bring products to the marketplace. *But is it?*

And what about those handheld devices we can't live without. You know what I'm referring to, and you might even be reading this while holding it – your phone! What version of iPhone or Android do you have, iPhone 10 or iPhone 35? The god of consumerism demands that every two or three years we buy a new shiny gadget, knowing all along that our brains will release the chemical needed to maintain our "shopping high." It's not that there's anything wrong with the one we got rid of, it's just that it's not the newest one, it's not the best one. Not to pick on any particular company or industry, but Apple makes a killing by selling us items to replace the perfectly functioning items we bought from them a year ago. People have as many as half a dozen older iPhones sitting wastefully in the back of a drawer, or worse yet, they were thrown out with the trash and are seeping heavy metals into nature. Heavy metals that could eventually find its way into drinking water.

And don't kid yourself. We have confused "consumeristic choice" with "freedom."

The funny thing about that, though, is that all of our so-called choices actually stem from the offerings of a very few super-wealthy folks. In other words, it's the billionaires and ultra-millionaires who decide which items they will offer us to choose from. Which smart phones or toothbrushes you can choose from is predetermined by the super-wealthy or the billion-dollar institutional investment funds that invest into a particular stock corporation. Apple or Android... choose!

The pharmaceutical industry is another high priest of the god of consumerism. They continually come out with more and more products that actually don't cure anything, and yet we continue to buy them! Their products *treat* us for symptoms but rarely cure us of anything. The stated goal of these Rx companies is to get as many humans as possible on life-long drugs that ease symptoms. In 2018, some marketing genius figured out a way to get over a million more customers in twenty-four hours. Miraculously, they officially reduced the acceptable blood count to determine who is a diabetic.

Millions of people went to bed, not a diabetic, but woke up with diabetes! Not because of anything they did, but because the god of consumerism must continue to be fed.

Millions of people went to bed, not a diabetic, but woke up with diabetes!

We are amassing more waste – and I'm not referring to our biological waste, I'm referring to throwing out perfectly good products because we have decided to buy the next big thing – faster than we can dispose of the old one. We are disposing of products containing every type of metal, wood, glass, or plastic more quickly than the earth can replenish itself. And it is killing us, literally.

The 8,000-Page Study

There is an 8,000-page study coming out in 2019. It was conducted across fifty countries over three years, and with more than 500 contributors. The United Nations backed it (they didn't do it). It emphasizes that human population has more than doubled on the planet in the past fifty years, from 3.6 billion to 7.6 billion currently, in 2018. And our human consumption of nature is occurring at a rate that is faster than the earth can heal and replenish itself. Water, forests, fish

...human population has more than doubled on the planet in the past fifty years...

... nothing in nature is coming close to replacing what we consume.

That's about eight-billion people who, on average, resting, take about sixteen breaths per minute. That's approximately 960 breaths an hour. That's eight billion people, resting, who inhale clean oxygen 23,040 times a day. That's about 184,320 billion gasps of fresh air being consumed a day. (Please, reread the number, it's staggering.) The report states that we are even consuming air at a faster rate than the earth can replenish it. Like most people, until you read Chapter 6, you probably didn't know how our very existence is directly tied to a microscopic plant ... phytoplankton. Don't feel badly ... if I had learned that in sixth grade, I had forgotten it, too.

The Canaries Truly are Dying!

Where's the panic? Where's the outrage? Is the language of nature as dead as Latin, so we cannot connect the dots to see that we may be on the brink of perishing ... as a species ... after just 200,000 years? Heck, dinosaurs lasted about 17-million years before the earth shook them off. Can't we do better than we're doing?

But the last fifty years have fooled us into believing we can live forever. The technology spike is no longer just a spike at moments in time, in history. Instead, we have constant technology. Consider the pacemaker, or implanted cardiac device.

Many who use a pacemaker live longer, yes, but they don't necessarily live a better quality of life. They just hold on longer while the medical companies continue to bill insurance companies who continue to raise the rates on us. People are living well past a hundred-years old, even though their last coherent thought was when they were eighty-seven. Can we not connect the dots? Or do we, as a species, serve the god of consumerism so fervently that we are willing to sacrifice ourselves for him?

I know people who have more than twenty-five pairs of sneakers. Oh, don't worry, they're not genetic freaks with multiple legs and feet, they're just consumers, like you and me. Go on Craigslist or eBay and watch people buying and selling used goods by the millions. Again, it's not that those items are broken or useless, it's just that they bought the next big thing, and now they need to either throw the one-year-old version away or sell it.

Marketing Masters or Devils?

If major corporations are the high priests for the god of consumerism, marketers are his evangelists. There isn't much interaction you can do in the world without having a company market something to you. While driving your car, or on public transit, you are bombarded with neon signs, billboards, and decals plastered on windows. If you look up to the sky in an attempt to get away from being marketed to, you're likely to see a one-engine plane pulling a humongous banner. Well, at least that's true at the New Jersey shore, where I spent much of my youth tanning and birding. If you read the newspaper or magazines, you can't flip a page without seeing an ad.

If you watch cable television, you are subjected to commercials. By the way, the U.S. Energy Information Administration's (EIA) most recent, Residential Energy Consumption Survey (RECS) stated there were 2.3 televisions used in American homes in 2015. Apparently, the god of consumerism has dictated that every person in the house needs a TV. If you think it's getting out of hand, don't fret, that number is down from 2.6 televisions per household in 2009, replaced mostly by small-screened handheld phones or tablets on which people now watch their entertainment. But ... where are those millions of TVs that were removed from our homes? Contrary to the apparent belief of many policymakers, they don't simply disappear. They, along with other perfectly-good-but-used products, become fodder for our growing number of landfill areas across the country.

You can't get on a social media site without being marketed to, either. Facebook marketers have become experts at matter-of-factly placing on your feed what you just searched for on Google. I can't even play a full game of Classic Solitaire on my phone without being pitched something for at least five seconds in between each *free* game. And how annoying is it when, many weeks after you've already bought your kayak – or whatever you'd searched for – pop-up ads for kayaks continue to bombard you for months afterwards?

The marketers have gotten so intrusive, our hand devices are always listening to what we say. Have you ever mentioned wanting a product and seen an ad for it soon after? That's because our precious phones are secret agents. For instance, *Siri* doesn't respond to you until you call *her,* but in order for *her* to respond to you, *she* must be listening. The term is called *Spyware.* We're consciously being spied upon, and we don't care, it makes it easier for us to shop for more stuff we don't need.

Solutions

If you were to take the wealthiest people of every major religion – the richest Christians, the most affluent Muslims, the most prosperous Agnostics/Atheists, and Hindu's – they each have enough money to stop the four-million deaths per year from drinking dirty water. The solution was implemented over a century ago in Chicago. We know how to chlorinate, and we know how to run cheap PVC water pipes. Why do we turn a blind eye to the poor people in Africa, South America, and Asia who are dying from dirty water? Think of the gross consumption in the Westernized world. We have all the money and technology necessary to eradicate death by dirty water all over the planet. Why aren't we stepping up to end those unnecessary deaths of millions of people?

That was a rhetorical question. I know the answer, and I suspect you do as well. The reason why: There's no money in it. The people who would be helped can't pay for it.

I'm a member of the Kiwanis Club. We worked in conjunction with UNICEF over a fifteen-year period to essentially wipe out iodine deficiency disease in the world. Every child needs to get about a teaspoon of iodine very early in life, but without it, millions of children each year have either died or suffered brain damage. Kiwanis didn't rant about it on social media, and we didn't stage marches so that people could think we are compassionate human beings, nor did we charge at windmills. Instead, Kiwanis actually did something. We raised about $110 million and built iodized salt plants in about ninety countries, using hundreds of thousands of volunteer people-hours donated by Kiwanis members all over the world. The disease that was impacting an average of two-million children per year is now gone from all but the most remote villages on earth. UNICEF has hailed this project as one of the greatest public health triumphs of the twentieth century. It was efficient. It was passionate. It was action.

Among the languages that have been lost, the language of caring for one another is becoming a ghost. People still talk about it, but it's hard to see it in action. The god of consumerism doesn't care if we care about others; he just cares that we care about buying more stuff. And we put our heads on the pillow each night and sleep fine, certain that our consumerism will eventually trickle-down to the destitute populations of the world and then everyone will be okay.

The god of consumerism has fooled many who hear about climate change, dirty water, depleting oxygen, the ruination of forests, and the extinction of species around the world. Regardless of what happens, we have blind faith that the next great technology will provide a solution. He has us clustered in cities because that's where the great jobs are, and that's where more money-making opportunities lie. So we don't hear the chainsaws ripping down trees, we don't see the funerals of kids dying

...we have blind faith that the next great technology will provide a solution.

from dirty water, we are insulated from the coughing noise of the asthmatic child dying from dirty air, we don't notice the extinction of species, because bats and insects are a nuisance anyway. So, we don't care. It's as if it's not real. We lock ourselves away in our tightly-sealed homes, not realizing we are dying from a slow drip of radon, carbon monoxide, and ignorance.

Did you know that every year many billionaires of the world meet up to decide where the economy is going?

In other words, they meet up to dictate where the economy will go. Can you imagine if the 2,153 billionaires, as listed in the 33rd Annual Forbes List of the World's Billionaires, decided to find ways to make money via the reduction of consumption of our planet, instead of how to make more money by consuming natural resources and selling stuff that becomes garbage within ten years or less?

We throw away trillions of dollars in phones with batteries and dangerous metals that leak into our environment. It's as if the uber-rich who profit from this don't realize they can make as much money with clean energy and by insulating homes to make them energy efficient. That's right. Imagine what would be possible if, instead of leading consumers down the road of yet another smartphone – that is only marginally better than the previous version – the wealthiest 1% looked at the forty-degrees North Latitude line that encircles the globe, and chose instead to rehab every existing home north of that line to make them 20% - 70% more energy efficient.

Those uber-rich, majority-share-holders of most corporations, have access to the policymakers and, even presidents, of those nations above forty-degrees north – all around the globe. So, they could convince the Congresses and Parliaments and Executive Offices to provide subsidies to the homeowners, similar to the U.S. rebates that existed for purchasing a battery-powered car.

Then, to finance the rest of the rehab, the local property taxing bodies could "loan" the money by increasing the property tax amount by a certain figure each year for 30-40 years (or the expected life of the home). The home owner would have to pay, perhaps, 20% of the total cost. Making those millions of homes more energy efficient would create millions of jobs over several decades, while still allowing those wealthy investors to put billions of dollars in their pockets (along with any other person who may own those same shares of stock in their 401k). And instead of being left with garbage (i.e. those six iPhones in the back of a drawer), we consumers would benefit from lower electric and heating bills. Best of all, we'd flatten the arc of consumerism, and end up using less of the earth's natural resources.

We don't have to depend on the uber-rich for everything. You already read what Kiwanis can do, so imagine if Rotary and Kiwanis and other similar international service clubs decided to help Cuba's sanitation system? Did you know that they, and many other countries, still use the ocean as their toilet? Can you imagine what all that waste over the hundreds of years has meant to the ecosystem in the surrounding waters? Cuba must import most of its fish that tourists consume. (Reread that sentence with the knowledge that Cuba is a tropical island!) It's entirely plausible that plants or sea creatures with healing properties have been eradicated from this world because of our crap!

The earth needs champions who are willing to make massive transformation. I'm not asking for a tweak, like in our education system. We've been tweaking the American educational system for so long, it has now become archaic in many regards when compared to the education prowess of the rest of the world. A former head of the Education Committee for an entire state in the U.S. marveled at how Abraham Lincoln, who served as a substitute teacher before being elected president, could come and substitute today. The main difference with him would be, instead of a chalkboard and chalk, he'd be writing on a white board with a dry-erase marker. That's what *tweaking* gets you, 144 years later.

We can't tweak our way out of this dysfunctional language barrier we have with nature. We need a full immersion, a massive paradigm shift.

Check out – www.theMEGAmovement.org to find out about Smart Consumerism.

Chapter 9
Citification: The Movement of Humans From Nature Into Cities

"The City was the acme of efficiency, but it made demands of its inhabitants. It asked them to live in a tight routine and order their lives under a strict and scientific control. There was no doubt about it: the City was the culmination of man's mastery over the environment. Not space travel, not the fifty colonized worlds that were now so haughtily independent, but the City."

Isaac Asimov, "The Caves of Steel"

Man has created an amazing thing – these cities. By collecting people together into a smaller area of space, we have been able to offer certain kinds of protections for each other. Municipalities can now clean wastewater and offer safe-to-drink water from everyone's tap. In fact, deaths due to polluted water have significantly reduced here and even abroad (which doesn't diminish the fact that about four-million people still die from dirty water in the world). Lives have been saved and humanity is grateful.

81% of the U.S. population now lives in city or urban areas, which make up only 3% of the total land space. And in the world, 55% of all humans live in cities or urban areas. That number is projected to grow to 68% by the year 2050.

https://en.wikipedia.org/wiki/Urbanization#/media/F ile:Historical_global_urban_- _rural_population_trends.png

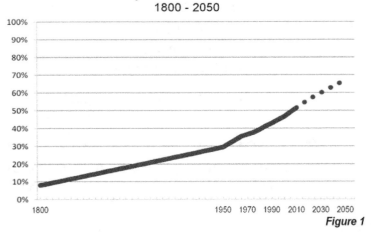

World Population: Urban Share
1800 - 2050

Figure 1

United Nations: 55% of all humans live in cities or urban areas, and that's projected to grow to 68% by the year 2050.

Earth Avoidance

For as many reasons as people feel they need to migrate to cities, whether it be for protection, jobs, security, or whatever else, citification is alienating us as a species from nature. We get up in the morning, our feet touch the man-made carpet or floor, and we begin our day much different than say, someone living out in the country. We prepare breakfast, get our kids ready for school, and then we get ourselves ready for work. Once out the door, we walk on cement paths to hop on local transit or get in our vehicles. Boy, do we love our cars. They are parked in cement lots or on asphalt driveways or streets in front of our homes, divided by a narrow strip of grass between the sidewalk and the street curb, which we try to avoid to not get our shoes dirty. We go to work inside another steel and cement structure, order food or go to a restaurant, work some more, go home to our families and the awaiting TV set or laptop, then go to bed, only to awake to relive the day over and over again.

Rarely, in our regular routines, do we interact with nature. Cities have done a masterful job of putting everything we need to survive – or to grossly consume – at our fingertips. As each generation passes, and as more and more people live in cities, our connection to nature continues to disappear. With each passing generation, and with each newborn child, our Nature Gap widens. It's no wonder there are fewer people than ever who can intelligently decipher nature's cry.

With each passing generation, and with each newborn child, our Nature Gap widens.

As I spent months traveling, while researching for this book, having gone from Illinois to Texas, Florida, Connecticut, Pennsylvania, Michigan, and California ...

wherever I went, people overwhelmingly agreed that just about every spot on the planet was experiencing a LESSENING of wildlife and biodiversity. Even Howard Stern and his trusted on-air radio partner, Robin Quivers, recently commented on Satellite radio that we are messing up the earth. I couldn't find, nor could anyone else, places in this country where animals and plants were actually increasing. In fact, the only way I found out about the wonderful Island of Misool, in Indonesia, was because since I couldn't find a place in the United States where nature was *winning,* I Googled, with hope, and found Misool, a place where human hands stopped interfering with nature and allowed her to heal herself.

There was a time when fishermen and farmers used birds to more effectively harvest food or fish. Fishermen once knew which fish were nearby by which bird dove into the water. Farmers understood which birds ate harmful crop insects, so they made sure not to harm the nests, eggs, and babies of those birds, allowing them to fledge and fly out into the world before plowing over a field.

The Horned Lark, once a farmer's best friend for feeding its young thousands of bugs, has been wiped out by an estimated 50% in just forty years. This magnificent bird is found in Alaska, every province of Canada, the lower forty-eight states, and parts of Mexico. The Horned Lark was instrumental to farmers, once upon a time. Farmers revered it for its bug-eating prowess. However, the absence of this bane of bugs in crops allowed insects to increase dramatically. Of course, more insects eating crops brought about excessive pesticides being showered over our food and some chemicals actually being injected into our food and eventually our drinking water.

A ramification of the added chemicals in our food is that much of it is estrogen-based. Estrogen doesn't play nicely with the male human body. In fact, a friend recently had to go to see a doctor due to an enlarged prostate. His doctor told him, and I'm paraphrasing here, "Estrogen may be the root cause of man-boobs and enlarged prostates. In twenty years, the percentage of enlarged prostates in American men has gone from 40% in men over 60, to the same 40% now in men over 40." Another ramification, one that concerns us all, is the increase of children being diagnosed with ADHD and other diseases or illnesses.

The Perils of Citification

There are perhaps, thousands of ramifications of earth avoidance and citification. With another one being the alarming rate of suicide in Japan, one of the denser human populations in the world. And, while many subconsciously or consciously believe technology can save us from whatever predicament we find ourselves in, it's important to note that, in Tokyo, arguably one of the most technologically-advanced cities in the world, where the population density is also one of the largest in the world, at about 6,200 people per square kilometer, they are investing over $1 billion to install anti-suicide barriers to all 243 train stations by the year 2023.

Hypertension, sleeplessness, anxiety, obesity, Type 2 Diabetes, and other disorders are off the charts in just about every major city. And while many may think we are living better than ever before, the percentages of unhealthy or sick people don't support that. And while many people think we are living longer than ever before, they used to be right, but no longer. According to the CDC, for the first time ever recorded, on the average, teenagers will not live as long as their parents.

One look at the data gathered on general population health and wellness over the last 100 years and the picture is clear; we have reached the top of the bell curve and we have leaped onto the other side, where we are plummeting downward, for the first time in human history.

For the third straight year, the CDC has reported a lower life-expectancy rate for the future of humanity in the United States.

For the third straight year, the CDC has reported a lower life-expectancy rate for the future of humanity in the United States.

The next chapter, *Nature Rx*, shows how we, as a species, can get off the bell curve and back to our pattern of increasing the next generation's life expectancy, which, by the way, some doctors believe could be approximately 120 years with the right amount of exercise, stress reduction, and a good diet.

The earth was made for us and we were made for it. Our *home* has always sustained us and allowed us to thrive, why are we changing it? Maybe you, like millions of others, need a reintroduction to nature and how amazing this planet is.

That's one of the goals of theMEGAmovement.org.

Chapter 10
Nature RX

"Nature is the best ... and most cost effective ... preventive and restorative Medicine."

Dr. Lauren Loya, MD (April 2019; Pittsburgh, PA)

"One touch of nature makes the whole world kin."

Shakespeare

"In the woods we return to reason and faith."

Ralph Waldo Emerson

"Walking in the forest is a low-cost way to deal with the public health crises of obesity, hypertension, Type 2 Diabetes, and all the other associated diseases."

Dr. Teresa Horton (April 2019; Northwestern Univ. IL, behavioral neuro-endocrinologist and evolutionary physiologist)

Riddle me this: What do Teddy Roosevelt, John Muir, Aristotle, Benjamin Franklin, Buddha, Thomas Edison, and even Neil Young all have in common?

Answer: While walking in nature, they all had revelations that impacted humankind in wonderful and meaningful ways. You can find hundreds of other people who, while walking in nature, had revelations that impacted the world in positive ways.

As Homo sapiens, our animalistic impulse to procreate in the wild has taken a back seat to our desire for comfort, entertainment, and tightly-sealed homes in which we take every step to keep nature out. In our never-ending search for meaning, happiness, health, creativity, and wellness, we have invented many pharmaceutical drugs, recreational (even illegal) drugs and alcohol, gym memberships, romantic comedies, and about a million other things. Are we living longer ... or are we just dying slower?

Because we spent 200,000 years evolving and adapting in nature, we are subconsciously more comfortable there. But our superficial and conscious avoidance of dirt, wet and musty clothes and shoes, bugs, bears, and snakes, etc. keep us in the silent, invisible, and slow death of indoors.

So, in droves, we left the small, quaint suburban towns, where we used to live among more trees than stoplights. As we already learned in the *Citification* chapter, most of humanity has opted to live in cities. Many for better-paying jobs and others for easier access to restaurants, public safety, and entertainment venues.

However, the Rat Race (the struggle to advance economically and financially in society) has caused a myriad of side effects. Use of stress and anxiety medications is at an all-time high. The amount of children diagnosed with ADHD has also reached their largest numbers and are steadily climbing. Suicides in cities in Japan, with the highest density of population per square mile, have reached epidemic proportions. High blood pressure, type 2 diabetes, obesity, sleeplessness, and other stress/anxiety related illnesses are affecting millions in the U.S. and around the globe. Heck, it's hard to watch TV without seeing an ad for a new billion-dollar colitis drug, as we are no longer living on the dirt, where humans evolved, to get many of the good microscopic bacteria that our guts need. What if I told you the answer to our angst, our health, our wellness, and our vitality lies right outside our front doors?

Use of stress and anxiety medications is at an all-time high. The amount of children diagnosed with ADHD has also reached their largest numbers and are steadily climbing.

In her book, *The Nature Fix*, Florence Williams observes that we are losing our connection to nature more dramatically than ever before. Thanks to the confluence of demographics and technology, we've pivoted further away from nature than any generation before us. At the same time, we're increasingly burdened by chronic ailments made worse by time spent indoors, from myopia and Vitamin D deficiency to obesity,

Thanks to the confluence of demographics and technology, we've pivoted further away from nature than any generation before us.

depression, loneliness, anxiety, among other stress-related illnesses.

ADHD-Attention Deficit/Hyperactivity Disorder

Dr. Victoria Dunckley, M.D., wrote an article June 20, 2013. In it, she cited scientific studies where children affected by ADHD went for a short walk in nature before each school day, or walked outside, in nature, before taking any test, along with examining other green-time experiences on children. They found nature is a viable therapy for kids with ADHD, and perhaps more importantly, even for kids not yet fully diagnosed with ADHD. She wrote, "*Whether a child has ADHD or not, even mild mental health issues in children can cause inattention, hyperactivity, and/or impulsivity. Here we have a natural intervention that can help avoid use of psychotropic drugs, promote overall health, decrease stress response, support brain integration and development, and improve psychosocial functioning. Green-time is truly a solid investment in mental wealth.*"

Thomas Armstrong, Ph.D., wrote an article April 25, 2018 in the American Institute for Learning and Human

Development, entitled, *7 Ways to Use Nature to Calm and Focus Kids with ADHD*. He concludes that children *need* nature and outlined seven ways to integrate nature and our school systems. By the way, this is for all children, not just those diagnosed with ADHD:

> 1.   Take fifteen to twenty minute "study hikes." Read from textbooks out in nature and, while there, lecture on key topics or review homework assignments.
>
> 2.   Schedule a class session outdoors. Sit out in a lawn or under some trees, and use the time to answer questions students have about the subject matter.
>
> 3.   Use a green, outdoor space near the school as the setting for doing a role play on a book being studied or playing a game involving academic skills (e.g. Vocabulary Tag – where one student chases the rest of the class with a vocabulary word, and the person caught has to give the definition).
>
> 4.   Plan a weekend camping trip for the class designed to bolster social and emotional skills.
>
> 5.   Before every test, have every student take an outdoor group jog.
>
> 6.   Allow students to take their writing materials outdoors for a creative writing assignment that involves nature.
>
> 7.   Study scientific topics by actually going outside the classroom to gather data (e.g.

information about birds, trees, plants, the clouds, wind, weather, insects, etc.).

Dr. Armstrong concludes this is how to turn Nature Time into Learning Time that will dramatically and positively impact ADHD-identified kids, as well as every other kid.

Andrea Faber Taylor and Frances E. Kuo conducted a scientific study published August 25, 2008, which proved that either rich or poor, black or white, students with ADHD did much better when walking for twenty minutes in nature, versus those kids who walked in either a neighborhood setting or a downtown city setting. Children with ADHD concentrated much better after a walk in the park, relative to any other setting.

My point with this is simple – nature serves as a safe, inexpensive, wildly accessible new tool in the toolkit of managing ADHD symptoms. Parents can jump for joy that they don't necessarily have to get their kids turned-on to a pill-popping habit. Please exhaust the option of nature before going the route of prescription drugs.

Hypertension = High Blood Pressure

According to the American Heart Association, 103 million adults in the U.S. have high blood pressure.

[https://www.heart.org/en/news/2018/05/01/more-than-100-million-americans-have-high-blood-pressure-aha-says] And, as published in the International Journal of Science, Nature (July 10, 2017), there are 5.3 million deaths per year, globally, due to physical inactivity—a number derived from a dataset of 68-million days of physical activity for 717,527 people from 111 countries across the planet. And nature walking consistently demonstrated a reduction in hypertension.

Sitting does the opposite. In a way, sitting is the new smoking. It can shorten our lives at the same rate as puffing away on cigarettes.

...sitting is the new smoking.

We don't want to bog you down with too many deep, scientific terms. But at the highest level, to understand how nature can reduce death due to stressful high blood pressure, it's important we understand the three divisions of the Autonomic Nervous System: the sympathetic, the parasympathetic, and the enteric. We'll focus on the first two here.

Sympathetic Nervous System = activates the "fight or flight" response. It causes a rapid release of adrenaline, which increases your heart rate and elevates your blood pressure, and it releases a surge of the hormone cortisol. While this process was built in to be a "good" thing for our bodies when we're confronted with stressful situations, the fact of the matter is that our modern, citified lives are making us constantly feel under attack and stressed, many more times per week than during our previous 200,000 years of existence, where moments of "fight or flight" were fewer and farther between. In our modern lives, where everything is marked by days, hours, and minutes, we find ourselves in a state of constant anticipation ... worrying about the next thing on our schedule, be it a project at our job, or racing to get our laundry before the dry cleaners closes, or having to drive over the speed limit to pick up the kids after school and/or get them to their competitive sports team practice or game ... or the one I've done myself ... rushing to pick up a prescription before the pharmacy closes. Ugh! And, this constant exposure to the "fight or flight" stress response causes a glut of cortisol that can disrupt just about every other bodily process. This leads to a myriad of health problems. During the time I spent with her in Pittsburgh, Pennsylvania, Dr. Lauren Loya listed these:

- Memory issues

- Weight gain

- Problems sleeping

- Cardiovascular disease

- Depression

- Anxiety

- Headaches

- Digestion disorders

Parasympathetic Nervous System = also known as the rest and digest system, it conserves energy as it slows the heart rate, increases intestinal and gland activity, and relaxes the sphincter muscles in the gastrointestinal tract. Simply by swabbing saliva from a mouth, researchers can determine whether a person is in a stressed sympathetic state or a relaxed parasympathetic state. And the science is proving that spending time in nature puts us in a relaxed mood.

Published March 2, 2015 online at the International Journal of Environmental Research and Public Health, *"Effect of Forest Walking on Autonomic Nervous System Activity in Middle-Aged Hypertensive Individuals: A Pilot Study,"* provides scientific evidence that a brief forest walk affects the Autonomic Nervous System and elicits physiological and psychological relaxation effects on middle-aged individuals with high blood pressure.

If, for whatever reason, you're stressed, do yourself a favor, take a walk in the wild side, go into nature. You'll be glad you did.

Type 2 Diabetes

The Center for Disease Control & Prevention (CDC; funny how the recently added word to the U.S. Government department's name, "Prevention," has not yet worked its way into the acronym, CDC), reported that there are actually more than 114

...more than 114 million U.S. adults with type 2 diabetes. diabetes.

million U.S. adults with type 2 diabetes. That's about 40% of the entire adult population. You see, they say there are 30.3 million who have achieved a certain level of the disorder that requires a drug to keep them from dying, but there are another 84.1 million who are pre-diabetic, and don't yet qualify for a drug to be covered by a health insurance plan or Medicare/Medicaid. And most of those 84.1 million will eventually reach the narrow range of blood-test parameters that will then be called full-blown type 2 diabetes, eligible for treatment with medication. This is a complex distinction to understand but allow me to try to explain it.

When we get a blood test in the U.S., and all of the results show that, in dozens of categories, we are within the acceptable range, that does not necessarily mean we are healthy. In the case of type 2 diabetes, for example, it simply means that *on average* those pre-diabetic folks are not yet sick enough to need, or deserve, a drug to help keep them alive. So, at 50 to 100-pounds overweight, but with the blood test results showing all areas within ranges that are *normal*, millions of Americans come home after a doctor's appointment and declare themselves to be healthy and continue eating donuts while sitting on the couch seven hours per day watching a TV, smartphone, or laptop screen. But read the obituary section of the newspaper, and you'll see more and more folks in their fifties who died *suddenly and unexpectedly.* Really? Is the death of a fifty-two-year old smoker who was more than fifty-pounds overweight and spent 93% of his time sedentary and indoors really *sudden and unexpected*? Hmmmm?

Dr. Teresa Horton, quoted in this chapter's title above, conducted the 2018 study: *"Walking Green: Developing an Evidence-Base for Nature Prescriptions in the Forest Preserves of Cook County [Illinois]."* Her team had a diverse group of participants take three, fifty-minute walks along a suburban sidewalk and three, fifty-minute walks along a forested trail, with all six walks occurring during a two-week period. Participants underwent different measurements, including blood pressure, heart rate variation, cortisol, fasting blood glucose, as well as a bunch of psychological tests. The participants took a ten-day rest, and then those who did the suburban sidewalk switched to the forested trail, and vice versa.

Dr. Horton said, *"We started this study with what we thought were healthy people. We didn't specifically recruit people who had high blood-glucose levels, which would be indicative of diabetes, but we had a small subset of people who started with high blood glucose levels. After these people completed their three walks [on the forested trail], they had lower blood glucose levels than even when these same people were out walking on the [suburban] sidewalk."*

When I sat down with Dr. Horton, she said quite conclusively, *"Sedentary behavior is leading to increased cardiovascular disease and type 2 diabetes. And while physical activity is good, doing it in the woods is much better!"*

She hopes the medical community will take away the importance of using regular doses of nature to reduce the stress in our lives. And she wants each of us to understand that, *"While most of us have an innate understanding that nature is naturally 'therapeutic' ... actual 'therapy' should be under the guidance of a professional, with a clear plan (i.e. a prescription) that leads to measurable outcomes."*

Spiritual Hunger/Mental Well-Being

Thomas Aquinas, a theologian of the thirteenth century, was also known as "The Doctor of the Church." He said God reveals Himself in nature. A few decades before him, Saint Francis of Assisi said we can see God in the mud and the worms. The Buddha is said to have been born in nature under a tree and then shared much of his wisdom while sitting under a tree. Native Americans revered nature, to such an extent that Sitting Bull said, "Every seed is awakened and so is all animal life. It is through this mysterious power that we too have our being, and we therefore yield to our animal neighbors the same right as ourselves, to inhabit this earth." In the Quran we find, "Do they not see the birds above them spreading out their wings and folding them in?" And the Bible recounts in Genesis the creation of the earth, clearly stating that humans were made by God on the sixth day... but birds came first, on the fifth day.

Vast numbers of people are turning away from the large religions of our world and are seeking ways to feed their spiritual hunger. Doing yoga with goats is a real thing, and meditation with water sounds has been popular for decades. My first real experience with the voice of God came as a teenager when my dad, brother, and I were driving our VW van on one of the most dangerous roads in the world, the mountain pass near Durango, Mexico. We stopped in a remote spot, all alone, with no man-made sounds to be heard. It was as if the trees and mountains were calling to me on the wind, "I am here." I can't say you will

I know beyond any doubt you can feed your spiritual hunger in nature.

have a similar experience. But I know beyond any doubt you can feed your spiritual hunger in nature. It's an all-you-can-eat spiritual buffet.

The Cure is Right Outside

I'm a substitute teacher of sixteen years, and it saddened me when I asked a sixth-grade class, "Why don't you go outside and play?" and one student responded with, "Because I can't plug in my game player anywhere."

There are hundreds of more studies from around the world that show many other health benefits from walking in nature. In Scotland, three hours per week for twelve weeks can reduce depression equal to or better than prescription drugs. In Japan, forest bathing is prescribed by medical doctors for a wide range of illnesses. In Sweden, wilderness therapy is shown to have as many positive effects on mentally-ill folks as hospital-based psychotherapy. In many parts of the world, researchers have even reported better performance on attention tasks when adults have a natural view from a window, compared to a man-made built view, or even after viewing photos of natural scenery compared to man-made settings. Clearly, nature helps us think, relax, create, and rejuvenate.

However, because our ego and consumeristic lifestyle can make us think we are separate from nature, we don't simply go out and get cured. In fact, as I was writing these pages today, a good friend of mine, who is visibly overweight, stressed, and lacking in vitality, said nonchalantly, "Nature is not really my thing," when I invited him to go on a few birding walks with me. It's as if he thinks we are separate from nature. We aren't.

The CDC reported, in December 2018, that U.S. life expectancy declined for the third year in a row, a disturbing trend, because unlike other periods of time in our past when diseases like cholera and typhoid and polio caused lower life expectancies, today's trend is due mainly to preventable issues.

[https://www.aafp.org/news/health-of-the-public/20181210lifeexpectdrop.html]

A slow drip of radon, chemical cleaners, and carbon monoxide is killing us in our comfy chairs within our tightly-sealed homes. We aren't really living longer; we're just prolonging death longer. Pacemakers and prescription drugs for the last ten years of our lives—is it worth it?

Let the MEGA movement help you get back to being a part of nature. After all, we are nature.

Chapter 11
What Now? A Call to Action

*"Unless someone like you cares a whole awful lot,
Nothing is going to get better. It's not."*

The Lorax by Dr. Suess

Eli and I are happy you've read up to this point. We hope we have imparted irrefutable data that convinces you of earth's plight. Our goal was to also make you aware of Earth Avoidance—(of not doing little things such as choosing to skip over a small patch of earth on the way to your car parked at the curb)—and for you to embrace nature more in your everyday life. We also wanted to share with you the ramifications of Citification; how living in urban areas—the concrete jungle—can alienate you from nature and make you sick.

We wrote about consumerism and how our spending habits lead to massive amounts of waste that doesn't simply disappear. In fact, it festers on top of itself, depositing harmful chemicals to the earth and its oceans. We touched on clean water, species extinction (at a rate 1,000 to 10,000 times faster than "natural extinction rates" http://wwf.panda.org/our_work/biodiversity/biodiversity/), and illustrated just 26 dots to connect in order to paint the picture that Mother Earth wants us to see.

Lastly, we wrote about how saving the earth is not a political issue in that one political party champions it for votes. Again, Eli and I are on opposite sides of the political spectrum, yet we came together to jointly share this message because it's not a political issue—it's a survival issue.

I'm not a "sky is falling" gloom-and-doom type of individual. After traveling to forty-nine different countries, I've found I'm about as optimistic a fella as I've met. Yet, I made up my mind to make it my mission to save our birds, forests, clean water, our planet ... and thereby ... save humans.

Sadly, 96% of the people who read "self-help" books fail at personal development, according to this article: https://bit.ly/2ZIRtFP. So, our fear is this: Although you might come to full agreement with everything you have read in this book, you still may not take *any* action. We didn't write this book simply to entertain you. We wrote it to provoke you into action.

Mavis Bates, a college teacher of Sustainability, recently said to me: "President Barack Obama said, "We are the first generation to feel the effect of climate change and the last generation who can do something about it." Our generation is also the last generation that can do something about the loss of biodiversity, the dead zones in our oceans, the desertification of our croplands, and the deforestation of our forests. It's not too late to save the planet, but we better hurry up!"

The first thing we'd like you to do is to join the MEGA (Make Earth Great Again) Movement. In addition to individuals like you joining, there are also many super non-profit environment organizations doing super work, and our plan is to break down the stovepipes in which they operate and get them to become affiliate members of the MEGA movement. With millions of paid memberships, policymakers will listen, since it would behoove and benefit them to do a better job at interpreting the detailed linguistics of the language of nature. Together, we can **Join the MEGA (Make Earth Great Again) Movement.** actually preserve and even restore the seven key areas of the planet. Let's leave our children ecosystems that produce clean, drinkable water and fresh, breathable air.

Six (6) Actions to Focus on

We are all, each of us and every person before us, in the last 200 years, complicit with how we got here. I, too, must fall on my sword. My avid birding and traveling hobby makes me a gross consumer of airplane transportation, rental cars, hotel bath towels and all the fuel needed to haul my 185-pound body of water and minerals around this planet just to feed my voracious appetite for nature. Quite a conundrum.

It's similar to the way Al Gore offered transparency when he was talking about his book, *"Earth in the Balance: Ecology and the Human Spirit"*, when he pointed out that he was working on his manuscript at times while riding in the back of a limousine with the air conditioning blasting. I've zigged and zagged all across the globe, adding to the pressures put upon our earth. So, I am a part of the problem. That's why I'm not pointing fingers. However, I'm also one to own-up to my shortcomings and work to make up for it. If I'm grossly consuming in one area of life, I must work at reducing consumption in other areas of our life. To that end, please join me in promoting these six ideas:

1. GO... SEEK THE LANGUAGE OF NATURE

45 Minutes: Spend up to 45 minutes a day with nature at least three or four times per week, on a dirt trail, and without your cell phone.

Fall in love with nature. French Aviator and Writer, Antoine de Saint-Exupery, once famously wrote: "If you wish to build a ship, do not divide the men into teams and send them to the forest to cut wood. Instead, teach them to long for the vast and endless sea."

Staring into your screen—TV, tablet, or phone— won't help you appreciate nature. You won't appreciate nature more by playing video games, sipping an over-priced coffee at your favorite café, or running on a treadmill.

When you walk into a forest, there are literally millions of different things happening. In just a few hours, trillions of buds on the trees change shape. Plants such as the Peony flower grow inches per day. Other plants, such as Sweet Alyssum, Calendula, and the Johnny Jump-Ups grow from seed to full-fledged flower in just fifty to sixty days. And the invasive Kudzu plant can grow a foot per day. With patience, you could sit and watch them move. The forest is always changing.

Learn to appreciate the tree, the classic nearly-invisible stand-in that has no spoken lines on the many stages where children's plays take place. Examine them and you'll realize that no two trees in the entire world are exactly alike. They are each unique like our fingerprints. The hanging leaves, the lines of the branches, and the millions of patterns in the bark make each tree original.

Join a local Audubon Club and go on some nature hikes. My own Kane County Audubon Club in

Illinois has several opportunities every month to go out into nature with others who can help you enjoy earth. I once led a group, and we got rained on, then sleeted on, and then pea-sized hail plummeted us, right before giant nickel-sized snowflakes gently cascaded on us. It was riveting! The participants saw Bluebirds, Phoebes, Meadowlarks, Woodpeckers, Wrens, Thrushes, and other wildlife they had no idea shared the planet with them.

I once took a group of soccer players on a nature birding hike. Although they loved playing outdoors on natural grass in city parks, the only time they entered the nearby forest was when they needed to retrieve the soccer ball. And, they feared poison ivy! I showed them what poison ivy looked like. No longer an unknown, they won't fear it going forward.

Upon hearing me speak about birds, one twenty-four-year old male said, "I never knew where birds went in bad weather." He assumed they must have a place to hide and ride the storms out. They don't. Why? They are a part of nature, just like humans once were.

Seriously, bird watching is the number one way Americans enjoy the outdoors. According to the "2016 National Survey of Fishing, Hunting, and

Wildlife-Associated Recreation" produced by the U.S. Fish & Wildlife Service, more than 45 million people watched birds around their home and while traveling. They also contributed a total of nearly $80 billion to the U.S. economy. Fishing was only 36 million people and hunting was 11 million.

https://www.fws.gov/birds/bird-enthusiasts/bird-watching/valuing-birds.php

And, birding has been found to be very therapeutic. See this article, and JUST GO BIRDING!
https://www.goodnewsnetwork.org/watching-birds-near-home-good-mental-health/

We are nature.

2.   SMART CONSUMERISM

Change the rate of consumption: For the planet to restore itself, we need to slow our rate of consumption.

We need to cut waste. For example, please try your best to see the paradigm in what I'm about to share. We have built machines to create machines that create the machines we use to sell a single one-ounce cellophane bag of potato chips in retail stores for $1.99, when in all actuality, there's only $.08-cents of food in the bag! Everything that makes up the rest of the $1.91 is profit and overhead expense. Instead of overhead and legitimate deductible IRS expenses, please try to think of those costs as waste. We've been taught to believe that it's an efficient delivery of product to market. That's ECON 101. I cry foul.

I believe in the ingenuity of young entrepreneurs to be able to deliver that $.08 cents of food to our gullets with much less overhead waste. The industry of the garbage of those potato chips is ten to twenty times bigger than the chips themselves. Ponder that for a moment. Then think of the thousands of other things we consume where the value of the actual item consumed is miniscule compared to the entire industry of delivering the item to us. It's simply not sustainable. By the way, this formula is almost identical for vegan food.

Prior to my TEDx Talk, which was a big deal to me and set me on the course to write this book, I went to buy a new suit. I figured this new phase of my life would hinge on the talk, so I went to some of the finest clothing stores in Aurora, Illinois. Upon reflection, however, I chose to go a different route. I walked into a thrift store and bought an eight-dollar suit and a three-dollar shirt and wore it on the biggest stage of my life. I resisted the urge of gross consumerism, and the audience was none the wiser. My opening line was, "This is what a bird watcher looks like." I was grinning, knowing I had repurposed someone else's fancy clothes.

Resist the false god of consumerism's demands of needing to shop for more—more clothes, more sneakers, more video games, more cars, the newest furniture, the biggest and smartest television set, the latest technological gadgets, and another wristwatch to join the seven you already own. Utilize Smart Consumerism. Not only will it grow your personal bank account, but you'll also avoid having those things become landfill in the near future.

We recycle only about 9% - 11% of all plastic. The World Economic Forum once predicted that if we don't stop chucking so much garbage, plastic will outweigh fish in the oceans by 2050. [https://www.weforum.org/press/2016/01/more-plastic-than-fish-in-the-ocean-by-2050-report-offers-blueprint-for-change/]

While this conclusion was hotly refuted and later determined to be impossible to authenticate, the optics and message provide a powerful visual. Who knows, if 90% of all large fish are already gone, which we have already learned is a viable estimate, then who's to say whether or not the weight of garbage in the ocean will be greater than the weight of all fish in the ocean (i.e.

remember, whales are mammals, not fish. Ha ha.) But seriously, regardless of the actual relative weight of our garbage compared to sea life, please remember, single-cell phytoplankton plants produce 50% of our oxygen. Choke them and we choke ourselves.

Each of us must recycle and repurpose feverishly!

3. PROFIT & LOSS STATEMENTS of CORPORATIONS

Corporations need to add Nature to their P & L Statements: The FREE water and FREE pollination labor that companies get to take advantage of, for example, need to appear on their Profit & Loss statements or else they will never value them. And therefore, we will continue to consume them at astonishing rates.

Consider a company that makes the chemicals for the dry-cleaning industry. If one of the essential ingredients didn't cost them a single penny, and therefore didn't appear on their profit and loss statement as an expense, why would that company ever try to use it wisely or spend any money to preserve it or capture it if it spilled? They wouldn't! It could slosh out of containers and literally go down the drain, and nobody would care, because it was free (and of course, once down the drain, some would end up in our drinking water).

According to Gallup, about 52% of Americans own stock.

 https://www.financialsamurai.com/what-percent-of-americans-own-stocks/

Yet, each year when we receive those notices of the annual meetings of stock companies, barely any of us go. It's time to go to those annual meetings in droves, and sign up in advance to speak at the microphones and let your voices be heard. Yes, we are complicit in consuming those $.08 cents of potato chips in such an inefficient fashion. However, if we don't change the paradigm so as to eliminate at least half of that $1.91 of waste within the next ten years, the earth may simply reach a point of exhaustion. We can do it!

4.   GRASS ROOTS ACTIVISM

Every environmentally friendly club has won battles but we're losing the war.

I've belonged to several environmental organizations:

World Wildlife Fund, Sierra Club, Ducks Unlimited, National Audubon Society, Chicago Ornithological Society, Delaware Valley Ornithological Club, DuPage Birding Club, Kane County Audubon, and even was appointed by the Governor of Illinois to sit on the state Endangered Species Protection Board, to name a few. So I'm sad to admit that, for as many times as we've won minor battles, which we must continue to fight, we've lost the war. From deserts to mountaintops, from streams to oceans, from small strands of trees to mammoth swaths of forests, simply put, biodiversity has gone down in just about every nook and cranny of our planet. Restoring and then increasing biodiversity is a war that must be won, or humans won't be supported and populations will shrink drastically.

According to the National Rifle Association (The NRA), they have nearly five-million members. And politicians will tell you they are, perhaps, the most influential and powerful lobbying group in America. But, imagine if we could all unite—bird-watching clubs, Kiwanis clubs, Save the Whales organizations, and every other environmentally-focused organization or person who is consciously aware of the plight of birds, mammals, forests, oceans, and clean air—we could easily have more than five-million members, from which we could get one-million of them to march on Washington and DEMAND reforms and changes to our laws and ensure drastic measures required to save our planet, millions of endangered species, and ourselves. It doesn't just have to be in Washington; people could march in Europe, Africa, Asia, Japan, and Australia and everywhere.

This is the MEGA movement!

5.   CHILDREN HAVE POWER

Children unite. Do not let anyone tell you that "someday" you'll make a difference in the world. Because you can make a difference RIGHT NOW.

First, imagine busload after busload of elementary and middle-school kids descending upon state capitals and the U.S. Congress to voice their concerns about whether or not they will have clean water, fresh air, or pollinated fruits & vegetables, or fish to eat. Moms, Dads, and Grandparents ... please make this happen. Your children's minds are not yet poisoned by our economic bias and the shallow, hollow, and vacuous language of consumerism that is riddled with mistruths and sleight-of-hand.

We adults blithely accept fake-marketing, such as a toothbrush claiming to be number one at getting into hard-to-reach places (when the truth probably is they just have more annual revenue sales than any other toothbrush; NOT the same thing), or a gasoline claiming to have the number-one detergent (God only knows where they get that claim from). So, before your kids are completely sucked-in to that empty void, let them testify in committees of legislatures. Your kids really do care. And they have enormous power.

My wife was the chairperson for an entire state's education committee. One day, she was in an elementary class of third graders. She told them she'd like to do an exercise whereby all the kids were to close their eyes for two minutes and imagine what they would do if they were each given a powerful magic wand, which they could use to do anything they wanted. Well, when they opened their eyes, did they ask for a million dollars? Did they ask to have fancy clothes or to look like a glamorous model on TV? No. Heck no!

The first nine-year old boy who raised his hand, stood up and said, "I would use the magic wand to get rid of all of the garbage in the ocean, because it's killing the fish my family needs to eat." My wife, with tears welling up in her eyes, called on the next little girl with her hand in the air. She said, "I want to get rid of suicide, because two people I know killed themselves." At this point, my wife, the school principal, and all the teachers in the room needed tissues for their tears. You, dear reader, now know that nature preservation is the answer to both of those magic-wand, youthful desires.

6.   ENGAGE BILLIONAIRES

If just a few dozen billionaires championed nature's cause, we could ensure our survival as a species.

I'm going to get real right now. According to Money Magazine, the richest 10% own 84% of all stock in corporations.

http://money.com/money/5054009/stock-ownership-10-percent-richest/

And the top 1% own about 40% of all stock. And if you want to get a feel for what it's like to be in the wealthiest 10% of all people on the planet, take a look at this website:
https://www.cnbc.com/2018/11/07/how-much-money-you-need-to-be-in-the-richest-10-percent-worldwide.html

So, instead of spending so much time and effort trying to get local, state, and federal policymakers to get serious about preserving nature, the greatest marginal benefit will come if we focus our efforts on getting the wealthiest 10% to convince corporations to offer us consumers more efficient choices.

There are now over 2,100 Billionaires, an increase from only about 400 in 1985. As drinkable water supplies are stressed around the globe (remember, we are depleting drinkable water faster than the earth can restore it and faster than our city water reclamation centers can make it clean again), the wealthiest nations will inevitably do a rush job and spend trillions of dollars to take salt, heavy metals, and dangerous chemicals out of our waters. We will have to waste an inordinate amount of resources just to have water.

But if five to ten billionaires agree now to step up and focus on water, that'd be the quickest and cheapest course of action. Now, the linchpin to this might be for them to figure out how to make it profitable and create jobs, but I'm sure they can.

Richard Branson is one billionaire who has jumped into the fight. VIRGIN UNITE is his non-profit foundation, founded in 2004. Since then, it has spun-off several specific efforts to focus on various ways to improve the world. For example, under the "Ocean Unite" arm of the organization, he held a large meeting on his privately-owned Necker Island, where they kicked-off the idea to preserve and help regenerate 30% of the oceans by the year 2030, that's the 30X30 call to action.

https://www.oceanunite.org/30-x-30/

And at the website of the airlines he owns, he has made it clear this is an essential part of being a good corporate-community partner.

https://www.virgin.com/richard-branson/why-do-i-care-about-protecting-ocean

The island of Misool Raja Ampat, one of the four major islands of Indonesia, is one of the few spots on earth where biodiversity is increasing. With a willing populace and strong government action to make it hands-off to humans, it was able to heal itself. In one short decade, 30% of the fish and shark life and coral reef have come back! We don't have to figure out the way to save our planet, the proof of concept has been markedly demonstrated. Earth can heal itself if given a chance.

So, we need more billionaires and more of the 10% wealthiest on the planet to unite around the other critical areas of the planet the way Branson is taking on the oceans: Water, Rain Forests, Northern Forests, Desserts/Grasslands, and the Frozen ends of our planet (i.e. the Arctic and Antarctic). Those five critical areas each need a Branson-billionaire to champion them.

Twenty Years

Many experts predict we have twenty years of life-as-we–know-it. If nothing changes or if we simply tweak a few things here and there, humans are likely next on the extinction list. Times are bleaker than most people could ever imagine.

We sit around in our comfortable chairs, chat away at our fancy clubs or restaurants, enjoy watching our children play soccer while debating if we should be keeping score or not. We shop more than ever before, many now from the comfort of our own homes and enjoy the *Free Shipping* and *Free Returns* from sites such as Amazon. Even with four-million people in the world dying from dirty water, we irrigate our lawn with drinkable water more than we should, just to ensure our grasses are the greenest in our neighborhoods. We vote on shows such as American Idol or The Voice, we gather in churches of many different faiths on specific days of the week, we put hours of thought into the next tattoo to blaze into our skin, in order to have a conversation starter, and we go about our existence on this planet in search of money, comfort, love, security, and happiness.

Meanwhile, we won't look ourselves in the mirror. If we did, we'd realize the ugliness of humanity in the eyes of nature and every other living creature on this planet. We are voracious consumers—killing for sport, for fashion, and for pictures on social media sites. We are wasteful consumers of clean water. We are irresponsible drains on energy. We are the biggest polluters and single largest threat to our oxygen. In short, we, who were once one-with-nature, in tune with her patterns and in love with her beauty, have become her worst nightmare.

However, you are not reading this too late. There is still great hope. Join the MEGA Movement! Visit us at www.theMEGAmovement.org and find out how to join your voice to the millions of other voices who are willing to stand up for the birds, mammals, trees, whales, oceans, clean water, and forests.

I understand you have been conditioned to not let anything intrude into your daily routine, but I don't know what could be more important than protecting your very existence, and that of your children. Should you have a platform, any platform, be it a school, a conference, a radio show, a television show, a podcast, or a magazine, please invite me to speak. Use whatever leverage you may have to save thousands of species around the world, including the human race.

Join the MEGA Movement

Wear one of our purple hats with honor (i.e. blue + red = purple; because this is NOT a partisan issue). Together, we can get the attention of policymakers and effect change. Together we can reverse our rate of consumption back to levels where we are not consuming faster than the earth can replenish. There is hope. We can figure this out.

In all seriousness, we must.

I am a hopeful creature.

About the Author: Vernon LaVia

Vernon has resided in Aurora, IL since 1998 with his wife and two daughters. He is the President & Founder of Defibrillators, Inc. (an AED sales & distribution company), and he currently sits on the state Board of Directors of "IL Audubon Society" and the Advisory Board of "The Conservation Foundation." He's a past member of the Endangered Species Protection Board of Illinois, having been appointed by the governor.

His father instilled in him the sense of journey, quite literally. Vernon has gone bird watching for over 49 years (since age 7) on 6 continents, in 49 countries and all 50 states. He has had many diverse experiences including studying socioeconomics in Costa Rica, observing bird habitat destruction in Kenya, participating in archeological digs at Mayan ruins in Belize, and building a Habitat for Humanity home in Central America. He's been as far south as Antarctica and as far north as Nome, Alaska. He's seen about 3,600 of the planet's estimated 11,000 bird species.

He attended Duke University where he graduated cum laude with a degree in Economics and minor studies in English and Classical Studies (U.S. Navy ROTC).

Vernon spent 1985 – 1999 in Employee Benefit Insurance Sales and Management at Fortune 100 companies, but he had a series of near-death experiences that changed everything. Suffering through amoebic dysentery and botulism while birding in Africa, and a 9-day coma/40-day hospital stay after contracting West Nile Virus from a mosquito while bird watching in Aurora, IL, made him realize a greater purpose in a life that had been mostly shallow, hollow and vacuous up to that point. So, he charted a course to leave Corporate America, own several small businesses that would be run by employees, and focus his life on three areas: local community service, human survival on the planet, and family.

In 1999, on his eldest daughter's first birthday, Vernon achieved his goal and left Corporate America to begin a greater focus on his family and community issues. From 1994 to the present, he and his wife have started eighteen small businesses and two non-profit companies. In 2000, his Dad died in his arms while bird watching on ATTU Island, Alaska, and from that death his defibrillator business was born. His wife Linda, former member of the IL House of Representatives and current Secretary of the Department of IL Veteran Affairs, has enjoyed the "journey" with him. Needless to say, he is also instilling the "exploration bug" in his two daughters, Veronica and Jacqueline. Vernon is passionate about helping human advancement. Life continues for him as a journey of discovery, and he hopes his voice will help others fall in love with nature.

About the Author: Eli Gonzalez

Eli "Che" Gonzalez was born to Jesus and Digna Gonzalez in Rochester, New York in 1968. He grew up in Milford, MA alongside his five brothers and two sisters He currently resides in the Tampa Bay area with his beautiful wife, Maria, and their daughter Trinity. His life is complete when his other children, Joshua, Mia, Alexis, and Isaiah come to visit.

As a ghostwriter, Eli has written more than eighty books for others, many of which have earned legitimate Best Seller status. He is the President and Senior Writer of The Ghost Publishing. In 2017, Eli founded the International Ghostwriter's Association. The IGA provides the only online course that trains and certifies ghostwriters.

Eli has served as a keynote speaker at some of the largest business or publishing conferences in the country. He also serves as an advisor to the Board of Directors for the Hispanic Chamber of Commerce, Tampa Bay, Florida.

To reach out to Eli Gonzalez to speak at an event, you can reach him at: Email: Eli@theghostpublishing.com

Twitter: @EliGhost1

When Eli is not writing, working, or preaching, he can be found walking on a beach in the Sunshine State alongside his wife and life-mate, enjoying another day God has given him.

Acknowledgments

God, thank you for everything. Thank you for the earth. I vow to be a better steward of nature and to help others do the same.

Thank you, family--my wife Linda, and daughters Veronica & Jackie. During the months it took to write this book, you were actually glad my mid-life crisis took the form of becoming an author instead of a shiny purple new sports car. But seriously, I am now even more in love with my wife and my two daughters, as your support and patience was moving and inspiring.

Eli Gonzalez, my co-author and new friend, I hope traveling on this journey of my first book was as rewarding for you as it was for me. A person cannot get to the next level in life without getting some new tools and new skills. Among other things, you kept my first book from becoming 1,000 pages...and thank God you did! Thank you.

Matt Hook, I owe much to you for being a stalwart sounding board and having to put up with my constant barrage of words, as I "tried-out" topics on your poor soul before tossing them into the public domain via this book. You steered me clear of some quicksand, for sure.

I'd truly love to discover more in nature with you by my side.

To his family, Heather, Micah, and Noah Hook, thank you for feeding me when I forgot to eat during many non-stop, eight-hour writing sessions.

Barry Cohen, Todd Birutis, Al Welby, and Jay Levija, no others make me spit-up laugh as much as the four of you. During many of our phone calls, I was actually out in nature doing research for this book, and you brought tears to my eyes with humor. But, is it considered humor if I laugh in the woods and nobody is there to hear it?

Dr. Teresa Horton, thank you for spending such valuable time with me at Northwestern University, Illinois. Your passion to scientifically prove the health benefits of nature is critical at this juncture in human history.

Dr. Lauren Loya, the trip I made to visit you in Pittsburgh, PA will be forever a highlight along my learning curve. Nature as medicine...drip by drip...is something you are utilizing in wonderful ways.

Mavis Bates, like a big sister, you often set-me-straight. Thank you for being generous with your time at Endiro Café, Aurora, IL.

Rudy Rodriguez and Dominik Lipiniski, thank you for being coachable coaches who coached me and were coached by me. Your youthful energy provided an injection of power at times when I thought my battery was dead.

Sherman Jenkins, Joel Frieders, and Ryan Dowd- -fellow authors in my community- - thank you for sharing the combined beauty and angst of getting published and trying to sell your unique concoctions of the 26-letters of our alphabet. One cannot get enough book-signing tips!

Mike Funkey, parting with wisdom during "coffee and cigar time" was greatly appreciated. And it was awe-inspiring to hear the stories about how nature is reclaiming hundreds of feet of your beach along Lake Superior at your Ontonagon, Michigan home.

Trevor Mitchell, many moons ago we had a long phone call, during which time the title for this book was created organically. Thank you for your part in helping to Make Earth Great Again.

Thomas Thorton, when you published your first book, *Serendipity*, it planted a seed in my mind that eventually germinated and flourished. Thank you for showing me what's possible.

Arthur Zards, the experience of TEDx Naperville has forever set my life on a different trajectory. Thank you for your brilliant coaching, and your child-like fascination when I demonstrated my bird-whisperer capabilities to get a Ruby-throated Hummingbird to come near us.

Terry Murray, we've spent hundreds of hours birding side-by-side, and I'm forever grateful for that time together. You were always more prepared, like a Boy Scout, ready for any surprise out in the wilderness. And I always fed you apples, bananas, granola bars, and an occasional Egg McMuffin. I was the winner of that bartered exchange.

Mike & Jan Baum, thank you for letting us stay with you in the far northern reaches of Wisconsin. The Loons singing on your lake connected me with nature's brilliance.

Bill Donnell, Charlie Zine, Sigi Loya, Bob Andrini, Theresa LeCompte, Josh Suliman, Wes Sadler, Joe Fazio, and Frank Binetti, thank you for knowingly and unknowingly being friends on whom I tried-out some of my material. Your questions produced clarification in my writing.

Bill Tannery, I think often about the twenty-four days we spent in Alaska. That was a time of great reflection 'on' nature while 'in' nature. It connected a lot of dots for me. I truly hope our birding paths will cross more intentionally in the future.

Uncle Mike Luongo, my half a dozen trips to California provided the opportunity to take you out into nature on many occasions. Your smile in the mountains, in the desert, and at the Pacific Ocean coast was always present. I will cherish being with you during the mass migration of millions of Painted Lady Butterflies in March, 2019.

Linda and Erik Thomas, when I was able to show your boys, Nick and Dylan, that Barn Owl just around the corner from your house, it gave me hope that the younger generation can still find experiences in nature that rival their video games.

Adem and Lauryn Aydoner, my nephew and niece, thank you for giving me a place to stay while conducting research in Florida. When the little guy is born, let his great-uncle Vernon teach him the language of nature.

Wendy LaVia Archer and Jay LaVia, my siblings, thank you for providing content and texture to my book and my life.

And mom (Johanna LaVia), thank you for your patience and understanding during dozens of phone calls. The fact that you and Dad were both teachers instilled in me the desire to share discovered knowledge with others.

Lastly, I know you are birding somewhere, Dad. My wish for you is that there are no "quivering twigs" in Heaven. Just birds that sit all day for you to "get-on" easily, baseball games where "your" team always wins, beer from British pubs, and Shakespeare-in-the-park every day.

CPSIA information can be obtained
at www.ICGtesting.com
Printed in the USA
BVHW081134100619
550592BV00012B/750/P